Jean-François Plante

Oils and Vinegars

Photographs: Tango

FIREFLY BOOKS

A FIREFLY BOOK

Published by Firefly Books Ltd., 2000

First Printing

Library of Congress Cataloguing-in-Publication Data

Plante, Jean-François
          Oils and Vinegars / Jean- François Plante.—1st U.S. ed.
[224] p. ; col : ill : : cm.
Originally published : Quebec : Les Editions de l'Homme, 1998.
Includes bibliographic references and index.
Summary : All about oils, seasoned oils, and vinegars, including recipes.
ISBN 1-55209-437-5
1. Oils and fats, Edible.   2. Vinegar.   I. Title.
641.6–dc21   2000   CIP

Published in the United States in 2000 by
Firefly Books (U.S.) Inc.
P.O. Box 1338, Ellicott Station
Buffalo, New York
14205

Published in Canada in 1999 by Key Porter Books

Electronic formatting : Jean Peters

Printed and bound in Canada

Contents

Dedication

To JoJo...

*For your great patience,
love of food and overflowing enthusiasm
for my cooking;
for your unwavering support
of all the somewhat crazy projects
that I am determined to accomplish;
for your quiet strength,
complete love and the laughter
that illuminates our path.
Because you are you,
thank you!*

The essential oil …

I must confess that, since I finished my previous book, I have eaten a lot, cooked a little, and indulged, without remorse or restraint, in a few great gustatory adventures in the land of tastes. However, I did especially miss you. Yes, it is true that we have had a few discussions about food, meeting by chance on a street corner, in a restaurant or in one of my shops. But, I needed more! I wanted to dream aloud of a world of pleasures and to share this with you. I wanted to invite you into this gentle harbor, created from the suggestions and ideas you have generously offered over time.

I wrote this book to respond to your questions regarding this bittersweet universe and, I must admit, to rediscover for myself this world that seemed so familiar . . .

Oils, vinegars, and the happy marriage of their tastes; I do not know everything yet, but I now know a bit more than I did. In these pages, rest assured, I will tell all.

Great! Sour grapes.

$\mathcal{U}$ntil just recently, the duo of "oil and vinegar" was a predictable couple with limited prospects: spirit and vegetable oil, vegetable oil and...vinegar. The only variation: different brands and bottle sizes. How original!

To the great delight of gourmet cooks, culinary sophistication has brought with it fine oils and vinegars, found on the shelves of a select number of better grocery stores. Then, the enthusiasm for Mediterranean cooking created a veritable tidal wave, a rush for green gold. Olive oil dips, wine tastings... acidic great vintages of *appellation contrôlée*. A small fortune is spent on vinegars, and on virgin, first-cold-pressed oils.

In this work, I review a fabulous world of tastes, colors and flavors. I paint a sensual canvas where the light explodes as much inside as outside crystal containers. A delight for informed epicureans and a reference for serious gourmets, this guide reveals the fascinating world of oils and vinegars. It is also an indispensable tool for the domestic cook who wants to create the infusions that form the basis of a simple menu or a cuisine brimming with originality.

Divided into two parts, this work combines two passions: oils and vinegars. It describes how they are extracted and produced, their nuances as well as their culinary and health virtues. Sometimes directly, sometimes while digressing, I offer advice and my own recipes for flavoring them, as well as some of the secrets that have contributed, if I may humbly say so, to the reputation of my own oils.

With this book as your guide, and your precious nectars as your travelling companions, set out on your own gustatory adventures and discover your own marinades and vinaigrettes, sauces and mayonnaises, grilled and fried dishes, pasta . . . and taste experiences!

Oil!

Oils

Oils

Extraction,
Storage and
Practical Advice

Sensual and enveloping, an indispensable part of our food pleasures, vegetable oil is all too often publicly denounced in the name of the war against fat, a very popular cause in North America. However, vegetable oils have more good qualities to offer than faults. It would be a tragedy to ignore the pleasures of a good oil in order to forgo a few undesirable calories! Allow me, therefore, to try to convince you of the delights these lipids have to offer us.

A little history   Used in cooking for millennia, vegetable oil has gradually become an ally of taste. From the beginning, it has inflamed the senses and excited the taste buds. The first vegetable oils were made from olives—a plump and tasty fruit, a veritable gift from the gods. The first traces of olive oil were found in the Mediterranean basin, and dated back to more than 5,000 years ago. This raw material, truly green gold, was a great priestess who introduced her followers to many of life's pleasures.

Light . . . and passion fueled by oil

Having served as a lamp fuel for centuries, oil has played a role in the arts. A source of light, it has participated in the creation of several of the greatest works by humankind. As an enveloping glow or an indiscreet witness, it has seen not only itself, but also passionate affairs of the heart, consumed.

With oil, the first corporal pleasures . . . and the most sensual

The Greeks and the Romans took baths in olive oil and carelessly used it as a miracle ointment for the body. Our ancestors ascribed purifying virtues to it; they rinsed with it, vigorously rubbed themselves with this nectar after their bath, and used it as a balm or an antiseptic soap. Olive oil also gave rise to the first perfumes. Floral and herbal mixes were left to soak and macerate for weeks in the oil. The result was—thrilling . . . encompassing!

Oil and some of the most beautiful sacred rites

Originally believed to possess heavenly and sacred properties (it is difficult to fault the judgment of our ancestors!), olive oil was included in the different religious rites of the three largest monotheistic religions—namely, Catholicism, Judaism and Islam.

Today, the oil still plays a sacred role during religious ceremonies.

From oils were born several of the greatest gourmet pleasures

After the many uses of olive oil had become commonplace, it was finally decided to introduce it into cooking, with the result that it almost miraculously changed the taste of food. This delicious lipid quickly became an indispensable ingredient. Tantalized by its sensuality, taste buds around the world trembled at this new conquest. It was used without restraint (apparently there were few weight problems at that time!)—sometimes as a preservative, sometimes for grilling, browning, marinating or frying everything that could be eaten.

In the course of new culinary discoveries, no doubt to appease gourmet cooks, new oils, originating from other oleaginous plants, appeared. Today, to satisfy a sophisticated food industry, an impressive number of vegetable oils can be found on the market, each one with its own par-

ticular taste and unique color, as well as its own dietary and culinary properties. Now, more than ever, it appears everything is going along swimmingly . . . in oil!

Extraction and Production of Oil

The methods for extracting oil have changed little for thousands of years. Even today, when high-performance presses and mills are available, a good number of oilseed-crushing operations still use proven ancient methods to extract their oil. For reasons of taste and quality, some producers swear that the old methods are still the best. On closer examination, it is hard to disagree. Nostalgia or reality? You be the judge!

First-cold-pressing in the Stone Age . . .

Long known as the only possible means of extracting oil, cold-pressing—simple, efficient and natural——is still the method most commonly used. The olives, seeds, beans or other oleaginous plants, which have been freshly picked, are left to sit for a day or two until they are bursting with sunshine and oil. Next, branches, leaves and twigs are carefully removed from the harvest. The oilseeds are then crushed in an enormous stone mill. This operation produces an elastic, viscous and extremely oily paste that can be evenly spread out on cylindrical mats——called "press cloths" and originally made from woven hemp——piled 20 or 30 high. These mats are crushed in huge hydraulic or manual presses—— care must be taken that their temperature not exceed 122° to 140°F (50°C to 60°C)——causing the magnificent and flavorful virgin oil to burst forth. The oil is then decanted, filtered and bottled immediately, according to common practice. This process produces precious extra-virgin oil: the most authentic, tastiest and most delightfully flavored oil that provides the best dietary, culinary and gustatory properties.

First-cold-pressing in the Stainless Steel Age . . . In response to the demands of progress, several artisanal oilseed-crushing plants have traded in their heavy millstones for screw presses. Made entirely from stainless steel, these small marvels shell and crush the oilseed in one step. Next, they extract the oil, without using heat, and reject the pomace, the solid residue left after pressing that is used as cattle feed or resold to industrial oilseed-crushing plants that will extract any remaining oil, using hot-pressing techniques. Oil obtained from stainless steel presses does not lose any of its purity, elegance or virginity. Hot-pressed oils, on the other hand, are scarred by the violent extraction method used to obtain them.

Hot-pressing With artisanal techniques, only 80 to 90 percent of the oil can be extracted from oilseeds. To recover a greater quantity (quality remains debatable) of oil from the pomace, a voracious (although not discerning) industry has developed high-performance pressing techniques. Concerned primarily with greater profitability, hot-pressing has little regard for taste. The oil is wrenched from the oilseed, using enormous, heated hydraulic screw presses. To maximize the yield, the oilseeds and pomace are steamed, using solvents derived from petroleum, to extract the remaining oil. Unfit for consumption, the resulting product, ironically called "crude oil" or "pure oil," must undergo a series of complex refining treatments. This oil is more resistant to rapid oxidation brought on by exposure to air or heat, but otherwise it is largely altered. Distillation of the solvent, neutralization, discoloration, deodorization, and even hydrogenation are all stages involved in the transformation and refining of industrial oils. The oils are heated to temperatures hovering around 375°F (190°C), thereby condemning them, according to many, to eternal tastelessness.

This rough treatment of lipids forever changes their fatty acids and leaves them lacking in vitamin E and mineral salts. These oils are, therefore, separated from their soul and, in large part, from their natural virtues. In short, hot-pressing will forever deprive us—this, to my mind, is the most lamentable result—of the singular taste of oils, their smells and their true colors, and, in the end, of the pleasures that they should give us.

Buying Oil

Do you waver between a commercially produced and a first-cold-pressed oil? You should know that, despite all the studies conducted to date, surprisingly little data have been found that ascribe more health virtues to the first, compared with the second.

If you value taste over cost, then choose without hesitation the first-cold-pressed oil or extra-virgin oil, both of which faithfully reflect the oilseeds from which they came. One note of caution, however: Always choose wisely. Take care to avoid the pretenders and insipid copies, for the designations "extra virgin" and "first cold pressing" are often not regulated. There are many ways to check for authenticity, but nothing can surpass your instinct and the sharpness of your senses. First-cold-pressed oils are recognizable by their taste, color and smell. Use your knowledge, infallible "sniffer" and taste buds, and you will be able to easily identify a true extra-virgin oil.

Storage

If you hope to give your oils more body and taste by storing them in bottles for several years, think again! Unlike wine, oil does not improve with age; it deteriorates, becoming rancid

within a few months, making its consumption impossible, even extremely dangerous. Fragile and capricious, vegetable oil does not tolerate heat, detests light, and oxidizes very quickly once it has come in contact with air. In storing your precious lipids, some precautions are necessary.

- Buy your oil in small quantities to avoid the need to store it over time.
- Choose opaque, dark or tinted bottles over clear ones.
- Keep your oils in the pantry or in the fridge.

Thus protected, whether cold-pressed or industrial, oils can be kept for many months, or even a year, and sometimes, if you really pamper them, up to two years. You can easily detect rancidity by the strong smell and bitter taste; discontinue the use of rancid oils. The gourmet's lesson: use them quickly to benefit from their freshness and their properties that will only diminish with the passage of time.

Use

Elixir of good health

Awash in the unjustified wave of panic concerning lipids that has recently hit North America, we have somewhat lost our bearings! Let's set the record straight. Vegetable oils are excellent, even essential, for good health. They are bursting with essential fatty acids that the body cannot naturally produce and that we must seek in our food and, therefore, inevitably, in our vegetable oils. These essential fatty acids are necessary for cell formation and hormone production. A beautiful conclusion, an argument based on taste and reason: not only are vegetable oils delectable, but they contribute to good health and help reduce cholesterol and, as a result, the risk of heart disease. Gentle lipid, true elixir of good health and taste!

Long considered synonymous with boredom and neutrality, vegetable oils have gained in taste and authenticity. With time, we have seen a stream of vegetable oils appear on the market, each one with its own virtues and characteristic properties. If, in the end, industrial oils are dull or indistinguishable in their taste, character, smell and color, cold-pressed oils reveal a whole universe of tastes. For unforgettable adventures, I leave it to you to choose your oil : olive oil for flavoring pasta and grilled vegetables ; peanut oil as a tasty base for mayonnaise or for frying vegetables, meat and fish ; sesame oil for cooking Oriental-style and for sautéing noodles, vegetables and seafood in a wok ; or hazelnut oil for producing a truly fine, smooth sauce for flavoring mixed salads.

Elixir of good taste

The World
of Oil

*I*f you believe that all oils are created equal, think again! Each one has its own particular world of flavors and virtues. Discover a few food phrases and anecdotes, then wander along different paths that will convince you of their own originality. Every good cook has been there.

To burn the midnight oil or pour oil

on troubled waters!

Olive Oil

Olive

A noble taste discovery that goes back to the beginning of time, olive oil still remains the preferred oil of gourmet cooks and dieticians. This precious consensus of opinion should be recorded without delay...Flavorful, exuberant, fruity, well-rounded and reflective of the soil in which it was produced, olive oil promises as many discoveries as there are varieties. If taste matters to you, choose extra virgin. It alone retains the natural fresh taste of the fruit.

Use

This all-purpose oil goes well with all your culinary fantasies. Cold and natural, or combined with a few aromatics, a little lemon juice or fine vinegar, it imparts a fruity and exuberant taste to vegetables, salads, fish and legumes. Use it as is on your food, like a sauce. Despite appearances, olive oil responds well to heat. Use it to brown vegetables or to grill meat and fish. You can even use it for some types of simple frying; however, keep the oil below the smoke-point temperature.

Virtues

Given the reputation of the famous Mediterranean diet, miraculous health virtues have been attributed to olive oil. On closer examination, these qualities are not imaginary. Olive oil is among the ingredients most beneficial to your health. Low in saturated fats and rich in monounsaturated and polyunsaturated fats, it lowers bad blood cholesterol and miraculously raises the good!

Storage

Olive oil, like other oils, must be kept away from light and heat, in a cool place, preferably in the pantry, in an opaque bottle. You can also store it in the fridge; however, when cold, it will congeal, although neither its taste nor its properties will be affected. It can easily be stored for one, or even two years. However, extra-virgin olive oil is more fragile than its industrial cousin, and its shelf life is much shorter. But, no matter how long it lasts, it is practically impossible to resist its call for more than a few days!

Briefly . . .

Polyunsaturated fatty acids: **9%**
Monounsaturated fatty acids: **76%**
Saturated fatty acids: **15%**
Degree of saturation when heated or at smoke point: **High**
Oxidation: **Slow**

35

Sunflower Oil

This elegant straw-colored oil, light, delicate, smooth and pleasant-tasting, offers a fine balance of tastes and can easily be flavored. Its finesse, affordability and dietary qualities make it one of the oils preferred by consumers.

Use

With its slightly nutty, fruity taste, and its mildness, this oil is indispensable. Cold, uncooked, seasoned with a pinch of *fines herbes* and combined with white-wine vinegar or with lemon juice, this oil is an excellent vinaigrette base for delicate and fragile salads. Lighter in weight and taste than olive oil, it emphasizes more than it masks. Sunflower oil is a delicious and subtle support for homemade vinaigrettes, marinades or mayonnaises. Multifaceted, it can even be used in pastry.

Sunflower oil tolerates moderate heat; it is perfect for grilling, but not suitable for frying. Although the pure oil reacts reasonably well to heat, first-pressed oil is rather fragile.

Virtues

Sunflower oil is among the best oils for good health and offers a fine balance among the different types of fatty acids. Low in saturated fats, it contains a good proportion of polyunsaturated fats, and a little of the monounsaturated fatty acids, although less than olive oil. Its use does not raise the level of bad blood cholesterol, but lowers it.

Storage

Sunflower oil does not congeal when cold, and thus can be kept in the fridge for more than a year. First-cold-pressed oil is more delicate, and its shelf life much shorter. Oxidation and rancidity will spoil it after one year.

> **Briefly . . .**
> Polyunsaturated fatty acids: 69%
> Monounsaturated fatty acids: 20%
> Saturated fatty acids: 11%
> Degree of saturation when heated or at smoke point: **Average**
> Oxidation: **Very fast**

Peanut Oil

Honest and generous, with a rounded, characteristic taste, a flavorful witness to its origins, peanut oil is among the most popular in North America, where the peanut culture is widespread.

Use

Peanut oil is without doubt the best oil for frying. Its resistance to heat and its mellow and singular taste make it the perfect ally for your fries. It is also perfect for mayonnaise. Light and crystalline in appearance, it can happily be incorporated into your dressings. Grill, brown or fry your fish and poultry in this oil: you will be seduced.

Virtues

Peanut oil is rich and high in calories, and contains a few too many saturated fatty acids to make it entirely and irreproachably healthy. On the other hand, the proportion of polyunsaturated to monounsaturated fatty acids allows it to inconspicuously lower the level of cholesterol in the blood. It is perhaps not the most diet-conscious choice of oil,

but it nevertheless has a certain charm.

Storage

First-cold-pressed oil is more fragile than its industrial cousin and quickly oxidizes. Since it does not congeal in the cold, it is highly recommended that it be stored in the fridge. Refined oil can easily be kept for a year in the pantry, away from light and heat, and even longer in the fridge, provided that the bottle has been tightly resealed immediately following use. Remember that air oxidizes all types of oils.

Briefly . . .
Polyunsaturated fatty acids: **34%**
Monounsaturated fatty acids: **48%**
Saturated fatty acids: **18%**
Degree of saturation when heated or at smoke point: **High**
Oxidation: **Slow**

Peanut

Canola Oil

Regardless of whether we call it "colza oil," the improved version, or "canola," for "Canadian oil," this is the new darling of dieticians. According to some, it is the oil of a thousand virtues. With a pronounced smell, it is a robust oil, with a harsh herbaceous taste and a hint of bitterness that somewhat evokes the flavor of walnuts. With golden highlights, this oil has breadth and personality.

Use

This oil should be used cold and uncooked as the base for any vinaigrette or mari-

nade. You can lightly warm it to brown vegetables, meat and fish, but avoid using it to fry. It does not tolerate heat well and gives off an unpleasant odor when it reaches smoke point.

Virtues

Everyone is talking about the virtues of canola oil. After much genetic manipulation of the oilseed, it has become, thanks to Canadian agrologists, the star among oils (until the day it is dethroned by another that will offer a more favorable combination of fatty acids for the body). It is even better for your health, say some, than the divine olive oil. Low in saturated fatty acids, canola oil contains a large proportion of mono-

unsaturated and polyunsaturated fats. As a result, its consumption simultaneously lowers bad blood cholesterol and increases the good. What more can you ask for?

Storage

Canola oil resists fairly well to oxidation; it can be easily stored for about a year, and even longer if kept in the pantry, away from heat and light. First-cold-pressed oil is more fragile than its industrial hot-pressed counterpart and oxidizes more quickly. Since it does not congeal when chilled, it is recommended that canola oil be stored in the fridge.

Briefly . . .

Polyunsaturated fatty acids: 36%
Monounsaturated fatty acids: 58%
Saturated fatty acids: 6%
Degree of saturation when heated or at smoke point: **Low**
Oxidation: **Slow**

Sesame Oil

Sesame oil, like olive oil, is one of the greats, with a noble and prestigious past. Reflecting the soil from which it came, with straw-colored highlights, this oil has a lot of character and body, a light aroma and full flavor. It is plump and full-bodied. Just like a great sauce, it will dynamically enhance all your meals.

Use

Thanks to its honest flavor, it will add a lot of character to your meals. It is perfect for Oriental wok cooking as well as for sautéing legumes, poultry and seafood. Sesame oil tolerates heat well; therefore, it is appropriate for use in frying noodles and breaded dishes.

Uncooked, cold, it is tasty in a vinaigrette for spinach and nut salad, on bean sprouts, or on broccoli salad prepared *al dente* and seasoned with a few sesame seeds.

Virtues

Not only does sesame oil offer an extraordinary palette of tastes, but it also offers a fine balance among fatty acids, thereby adding to its reputation and making it one of the most virtuous oils. Its level of saturated fatty acids is sufficiently low to allow polyunsaturated and monounsaturated fats to coexist in harmony. Consumption of this oil simultaneously reduces bad blood cholesterol and increases good cholesterol.

Storage

Sesame oil is fairly resistant to oxidation. However, as it does not congeal when

chilled, it may be best to store it in the fridge to pamper it a little and thereby maximize its shelf life.

Briefly . . .
Polyunsaturated fatty acids: **44%**
Monounsaturated fatty acids: **41%**
Saturated fatty acids: **15%**
Degree of saturation when heated or at smoke point: **High**
Oxidation: **Average**

Sesame

Grapeseed Oil

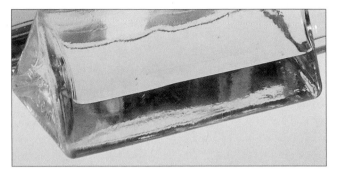

A light, limpid and fluid oil with soft green highlights, grapeseed oil resists heat well and happily adopts other flavors.

Use

This delightfully creamy oil is superb for all types of grilling. Flavor it using a blend of *fines herbes* and aromatics, and *voilà*, the perfect oil for your beef fondue. Its obvious lightness makes it an extraordinary oil for delicate mixed salads. It is highly recommended for marinating meat and poultry, both of which it is able to easily penetrate and tenderize.

Virtues

Without being virtue incarnate, grapeseed oil can nonetheless be classed among high-quality oils. With its low level of saturated fatty acids, a good measure of polyunsaturated fats and a respectable dose of monounsaturated fats, grapeseed oil offers a good dietary balance. Moderate consumption of this oil contributes to the lessening of bad blood cholesterol.

Storage

Grapeseed oil is rather fragile and oxidizes rapidly. Since it does not congeal when chilled, it is highly recommended that it be stored in the fridge, where its shelf life can easily reach one year. It is, however, preferable that the bottle be tightly resealed after use, in order to prevent any oxidation.

Briefly . . .
Polyunsaturated fatty acids: **69.9%**
Monounsaturated fatty acids: **16.1%**
Saturated fatty acids: **9.6%**
Degree of saturation when heated or at smoke point: **High**
Oxidation: **Quick**

Grapeseed

Soya Oil

Made from soya beans, soya oil is delicate, neutral, light and crystalline. With no discernible taste, it serves as a discreet base for food. It contributes indirectly to the creation of a high-quality condiment. In effect, by using soya pomace mixed with soya beans, the Japanese prepare with care and knowhow the irreplaceable tamari sauce.

Use

Soya oil does not tolerate heat well; therefore, it is better to use it cold. Its neutral, silky and light taste is ideal as a light base for dressings or marinades. Its clarity and refinement make it a chameleon lipid that easily absorbs the flavors of *fines herbes* and aromatics.

Virtues

Its low level of saturated fat makes soya oil healthy. As it has fairly high levels of polyunsaturated and mono-unsaturated fats, it can reduce bad blood cholesterol.

Storage

This oil tolerates the cold and, unlike olive oil, does not congeal in the fridge. Easily oxidized, especially when first-pressed, it requires a minimum amount of cooling to prolong its shelf life. Protected from both heat and light, it will remain fresh for more than a year.

Briefly...
Polyunsaturated fatty acids: **58%**
Monounsaturated fatty acids: **24%**
Saturated fatty acids: **15%**
Degree of saturation when heated or at smoke point:
Average
Oxidation: **Average**

Anchoyade oil

Saffron oil

Fines herbes oil

Pomodoro oil

Oriental flavored oil

Citrus oil

mushroom oil

r oil

il

Flavored *Oils*

Essentially, all oils can be transformed into veritable tasteful flowers of flavor when combined with spices and aromatics in measured quantities. Flavored oils can be prepared hot or cold in the blink of an eye. Simply use your imagination or use my secrets, but always use the oils with care and a little patience. If you do, they will subtly enhance your cooking, to the great delight of all your guests.

Anchoyade oil

Anchoyade Oil

This superb oil is flavored with herbs, garlic and anchovies.
Reflecting the colors of Provence, this oil will add flavor and character
to your grilled dishes, pastas and pizzas.

2 cups (500 mL)	**Pure olive oil**
1 tin (48 g)	**Anchovy fillets**
4 tbsp (20 g)	***Herbes de Provence***
4	**Garlic cloves**
2	**Bay leaves**
	Sprigs of dried rosemary, as a garnish

Even if you do not like anchovies, do not deprive yourself of this delicious oil... Leave them out of the recipe and it will still be magnificent.

In a thick-bottomed saucepan, gently heat the oil and the other ingredients over medium heat, until the oil begins to lightly sizzle. Heat for 1 to 2 minutes, but avoid frying. Remove from heat and let cool. Next, strain this infusion through a fine sieve or through two or three thicknesses of cheesecloth, to save the crystalline and flavored oil. Empty it into a very clean bottle or jar. Garnish the bottle with a few sprigs of dried rosemary and store this flavored potion in the fridge.

Recipes

Stuffed Squid

Marinated Mushrooms à l'italienne

Pork Chops à la portugaise

Anchoyade Spaghetti

Other suggestions

Grilled Pepper Salad

Homemade Tapenade

Pissaladière

Eggplant Caviar

Ratatouille

Anchoyade Croutons

Coquilles Saint-Jacques à la provençale

Truffle Oil

The honest and powerful taste of truffle gives this oil a lot of panache. With its strong, wild taste, truffle oil will happily enliven your otherwise plain pasta, omelettes and grilled dishes.

2 cups (500 mL)	**Pure olive oil**
3	**Black truffles**

Recipes

Truffle-flavored Filet Mignon

Warm Chicken Liver Salad with Truffles and Vinegar

Omelette with Black Truffles

Other suggestions

Pork Chops with Mushrooms

Calf's Liver with Oyster Mushrooms

Duck Breast with Truffles

Escargots with Fines herbes and Mushrooms

Chicken Liver Terrine

First, finely slice the truffles. Add them to the olive oil and mix lightly, using a fork. Let macerate at least 3 weeks in the pantry in a bottle or very clean glass jar. Remember to shake the container every so often. Next, filter through a fine sieve or through two or three thicknesses of muslin. Garnish with a small slice of truffle. Store the oil in a bottle or in a very clean jar, in the fridge.

Pomodoro Oil

With its color of sun-dried tomatoes and flavor of oregano, this oil will become an ideal ally for all your dishes with a southern European flavor. You will have all the exuberance of Italy in a bottle. Delicious on pasta, grilled dishes, bruschetta, panini and pizzas. Pure rapture...

1 0	**Sun-dried tomatoes**
2 cups (500 mL)	**Pure olive oil**
1 tbsp (15 mL)	**Lemon juice**
6 tbsp (30 g)	**Dried oregano**
4	**Garlic cloves, grilled**

Recipes

Tagliatelle Salad with Tomato Coulis

Grilled Snapper Fillets with Dried Tomatoes

Grilled Eggplant and Fresh Tomato Salad with Bocconcini

Other suggestions

Fusilli with Sun-dried Tomatoes and Parma Ham

Fresh Pasta Salad with Tomato Coulis

Rigatoni with Sun-dried Tomatoes and Grilled Vegetable Fricassee

Bruschetta with Fresh Tomatoes and Bocconcini

Rehydrate the sun-dried tomatoes by soaking them in a little warm water and lemon juice for approximately 30 minutes. Next, dry them with a paper towel. Combine the tomatoes, oil and other ingredients in a blender, and pulse to avoid emulsifying as that will make it impossible to decant the mixture. Next, filter the mixture twice through a fine sieve or through two or three thicknesses of cheese-cloth. Set aside the tomato purée in the fridge in a small tightly sealed container for use with pasta or fish. Let the infused oil marinade in the pantry for 2 weeks. Filter again, keeping only the flavored, orange-tinted, transparent oil. Pour the oil into a very clean bottle or jar. Store in the fridge.

Oriental-Flavored Oil

*This is a spellbinding oil, a complex mix, rich and balanced.
Its unique flavors will make you dream of travel... It will leave
its mark on your vegetables, meats and fish sautéed in the wok. It will
also happily marinate your chicken breasts. It will even, oh
miracle of miracles, give your sad tofu some flavor...*

2 cups (500 mL)	**Soya oil**
2 tbsp (10 g)	**Fresh ginger, grated**
4 pieces	**Star anise, lightly crushed**
1 tbsp (15 g)	**Coriander seeds, lightly crushed**
3	**Garlic cloves, minced**
2 tbsp (10 g)	**Crushed chilis**

Thoroughly combine the oil and the other ingredients, mixing with a fork or a whisk, and let steep and infuse for 3 weeks in the refrigerator. Next, filter, using a fine sieve. Pour the oil into a very clean bottle or container, and garnish, if so desired, with a few coriander seeds, star anise and dried ginger root. Store in the fridge.

Saffron Oil

Saffron Oil

*This fine and subtle oil will enhance
the flavor of your fish and seafood, chicken,
rabbit or small game.*

2 cups (500 mL)	Sunflower oil
3 tsp (15 g)	Saffron
3	Small garlic cloves, minced
	Saffron threads, as a garnish

In a thick-bottomed saucepan, gently heat the oil and other ingredients until everything begins to sizzle. Cook another 2 minutes; avoid frying. Remove from heat. Let cool and infuse. Filter through a fine sieve or through two or three thicknesses of cheesecloth, lightly squeezing to extract the flavor, aroma and color. Pour the oil into a very clean bottle or jar. Store in the fridge.

Recipes

Saffron Seviche

Risotto à la milanaise

Shrimp and Pasta Salad with Saffron Oil

Other suggestions

Chicken Saffron Aiguillettes

Saffron Mayonnaise

Mussels in Saffron Cream Sauce

Fines herbes and Shallot Oil

This oil has a characteristic taste
that evokes flavors from the garden. Invigorating and
fresh, it will enliven all your vegetable,
pasta and salad dishes.

2 cups (500 mL)	**Canola oil**
4	**Shallots, minced**
6	**Green onions, minced**
4	**Rosemary sprigs**
6	**Thyme sprigs**
8	**Fresh sage leaves**

Recipes

Pork Paillards with
Fines herbes

Chicken Breasts with
Parma Ham

Crispy Pork Medallions
with Fines herbes

Other suggestions

Cold Pasta Salad with
Tuna and Red Onion

Small Potatoes with
Shallots and
Herbes de Provence

In a thick-bottomed saucepan, gently heat the oil and the other ingredients until everything begins to lightly sizzle. Heat for 2 minutes; avoid frying. Remove from heat and let infuse, stand and cool. Filter through a fine sieve or through two or three thicknesses of cheesecloth, and lightly squeeze to extract the maximum amount of flavor. Pour into a very clean bottle or jar. Store the flavored and crystalline oil in the pantry or fridge.

Fines herbes oil

Tex-Mex oil

Tex-Mex Oil

Surprising and explosive, this oil offers a fine balance of spicy and scented flavors. It will give character and spirit to your Tex-Mex dishes. A superb oil for marinating chicken breasts and steaks, and for seasoning bruschetta, grilled fish, seviche, guacamole and chili.

2 cups (500 mL)	**Peanut oil**
4	**Small jalapeño peppers, minced**
4	**Garlic cloves, minced**
2 tbsp (10 g)	**Crushed chilis**
	Dried chili peppers and cinnamon stick, as a garnish

In a thick-bottomed saucepan, gently heat the oil and the other ingredients until everything begins to lightly sizzle. Cook for another 2 minutes; avoid frying. Remove from heat; let stand and cool. Filter through a fine sieve or through two or three thicknesses of cheesecloth, lightly squeezing to extract all the aromas and flavors. Pour into a very clean bottle or jar. Store the flavored and crystalline oil in the pantry or fridge. Garnish with a few dried chili peppers and a stick of cinnamon if so desired.

Recipes

Tex-Mex Chicken Thighs

Tuna Steaks with Fruit Salsa

Pork Brochettes with Santa Fe Peanuts

Other suggestions

Beef Chili with Peppers

Chicken Fajitas with Shallots

Onion Focaccia

Spicy Chickpea Salad with Fresh Coriander

Porcini Mushroom Oil

The porcini mushrooms will imbue this olive oil with their honest taste. With body and a solid soul, it lends itself to numerous culinary exercises: It is ideal for marinating red meat, for brushing on grilled dishes and for sautéing mushrooms and vegetables.

2 cups (500 mL)	**Olive oil**
4 tbsp (90 g)	**Dried porcini mushrooms (or ceps)**

Recipes

Rigatoni with Porcini Mushrooms, Rosa Sauce

Veal Escalopes with a Cheese–Mushroom Duo

Chicken and Mushroom Panini

Other suggestions

Beef Flank with Mushrooms

Sautéed Oyster Mushrooms

Onion and Mushroom Fricassee

Grilled Squid Stuffed with Mushrooms

Chicken Breasts with Oyster Mushrooms

In a thick-bottomed saucepan, gently heat the oil and mushrooms until sizzling. Cook for another 2 minutes; avoid frying. Remove from heat. Let stand and cool. Next, in a food processor, combine the ingredients and pulse to avoid emulsifying, which would make it impossible to decant the mixture. Filter through a fine sieve or through two or three thicknesses of cheesecloth. Pour into a very clean bottle or jar. Store the flavored and crystalline oil in the fridge or pantry.

Pepper oil

Pepper Oil

Here is a surprising and intoxicating recipe. The grilled peppers provide a singular taste to this oil infusion. Enhanced with oregano and shallots, its flavor is perfect! Use it without restraint on your grilled vegetables, pasta and fish, or even as a well-rounded vinaigrette for your salad.

2	**Red peppers, grilled**
1	**Yellow pepper, grilled**
2 cups (500 mL)	**Sunflower oil**
3 tbsp (15 g)	**Dried oregano**
2	**Green onions, minced**

First, halve, then stem and seed the peppers. Grill them in the oven or on the barbecue for about 15 minutes, until the skin begins to blacken and blister. Remove the grilled skin, saving only the flesh. In a thick-bottomed saucepan, gently heat the oil and the other ingredients until everything begins to sizzle. Cook for another 2 minutes; avoid frying. Remove from heat, let stand and cool. Next, using a food processor, pulse the mixture to avoid emulsifying, which would make it impossible to decant the mixture. Filter twice through a fine sieve or through two or three thicknesses of cheesecloth, lightly squeezing to extract all the aromas and flavors. Let steep and decant in the fridge for 3 to 4 days, then filter again, keeping only the crystalline oil. Use immediately, or store in the fridge in a very clean bottle or jar.

Recipes

Fusilli with Salmon and Red Pepper

Fresh Mussel Salad with Peppers and Green Onions

Veal Shank with Peppers

Other suggestions

Cold Grilled Squid Salad

Olive Bruschetta

Eggplant Gratin with Pepper Coulis

Veal Escalope with Olive, Pepper and Onion Fricassee

Goat's Milk Cheese and Pistachio Pizza

Citrus Oil

*This fruity and slightly acidic oil will enchant you
with its lightness. The sweetness of the dill magnificently counterbalances
the exuberance of the citrus fruit. It is an ideal companion for your salads
and provides a delicious base for your grilled fish marinade. It will also
gently and subtly enhance the taste of your seafood.*

2 cups (500 mL)	Grapeseed oil
1	Large bunch of fresh dill
1	Orange (zest)
1	Lemon (zest)
1	Lime, finely sliced
2 tbsp (30 g)	Dill seeds

Recipes

Roasted Salmon Fillets

Chicken Breasts Stuffed
with Dried Tomatoes and
Kalamata Olives

West Coast Couscous

Other suggestions

Grilled Fish with Citrus Fruit

Greek Salad with
Greek Feta Cheese

Avocado Vinaigrette with Capers

Tabbouleh with Citrus Fruit

Spinach Salad with Goat's Milk
Cheese and Citrus Fruit

Fresh Asparagus with
Lemon and Coriander

In a thick-bottomed saucepan, gently heat the oil and the other ingredients until everything begins to sizzle. Cook for 2 minutes; avoid frying. Remove from heat, let stand and cool. Next, filter through a fine sieve or through two or three thicknesses of cheesecloth, squeezing the condiments to extract all the aromas and flavors. Pour into a very clean bottle or jar and store in the fridge or pantry. Let steep in the fridge for 3 to 4 days, then filter again, keeping only the crystalline oil. Use immediately, or store in the fridge in a very clean bottle or jar.

Recipes

How to **Flavored**

Use **Oils**

By following my suggestions and adding your imagination, you have now prepared oils that are as delicious as they are beautiful. Following are a few simple recipes that are quick to prepare, but full of taste and surprises. It is up to me to suggest them, you to benefit from them, and all of us to enjoy them!

Roasted Salmon Fillets

with Citrus Oil

¹/₃ cup (70 mL)	**Citrus oil**
1	**Lemon (juice and zest)**
2 tbsp (10 g)	**Fresh dill, finely chopped**
4 tbsp (60 mL)	**Tamari or soya sauce**
To taste	**Salt and ground pepper**
4 x 5 oz (150 g)	**Atlantic salmon fillets**

Prepare the marinade by using a whisk to combine the oil, lemon juice, dill and tamari. Season with salt and pepper. Place the salmon fillets in the marinade and let sit in the fridge for 1 hour.

Preheat a skillet over high heat, and sear the salmon fillets for 2 minutes maximum on each side, starting with the skin side. Cook until the skin is crispy and the flesh pink and soft.

Serve on a nest of grilled vegetables. Lightly cover with warm marinade.

Chicken Breasts Stuffed with
Sun-Dried Tomatoes and Kalamata Olives

5	**Sun-dried tomatoes**
12	**Kalamata olives, pitted**
1	**Orange (zest and juice)**
1	**Lime (zest and juice)**
4 x 5 oz (150 g)	**Chicken breasts**
1/3 cup (80 mL)	**Citrus oil**
1 tsp (3 g)	**Fresh or dried herbs**
To taste	**Salt and ground pepper**

West Coast Couscous

3 cups (600 g)	**Couscous**
1/4 cup (60 mL)	**Citrus oil**
1	**Green onion, finely chopped**
1/2 cup (approx. 65 g)	**Red bell pepper, diced**
1/2 cup (approx. 65 g)	**Mango, diced**
1/2 cup (approx. 65 g)	**Zucchini, diced**
1/3 cup (30 g)	**Currants**
1	**Orange (zest)**
1	**Bunch of fresh parsley, chopped**
To taste	**Salt and ground pepper**

Finely chop the sun-dried tomatoes, olives, orange and lime zests. Combine all the ingredients into a stuffing and set aside. With a knife, make a deep cut into each chicken breast. Using a pastry bag or a spoon, fill the chicken with the stuffing. Prepare a marinade from the oil, orange and lime juice, fresh or dried herbs and ground pepper. Marinate for at least 2 hours in the fridge. In a preheated skillet, sear the chicken breasts over medium heat for 5 to 7 minutes.

Slice each portion into fine escalopes and garnish with a few olives. Serve with the fresh-fruit couscous, and the vegetables prepared *al dente*.

You will love it! To prepare the couscous, carefully combine the ingredients using a fork. You will be seduced by the result: a sweet, fruity and magnificently flavored couscous.

Stuffed Squid

with Anchoyade

8	**Small squid**
1	**Small onion**
1	**Bunch of Italian parsley, chopped**
2	**Garlic cloves**
¼ cup (50 g)	**Breadcrumbs**
¼ cup (60 mL)	**Anchoyade oil**
1	**Lemon (juice)**
To taste	**Salt and ground pepper**
1	**Pinch of *herbes de Provence***

*T*horoughly clean the squid, body and tentacles. If you are running short of time, buy deep-frozen squid that have already been trimmed. Prepare the stuffing. Finely chop the onion, parsley, garlic, *herbes de Provence* and the tentacles. Add the breadcrumbs, and combine all the ingredients. Using a pastry bag or a spoon, insert the stuffing into each squid and seal the opening with a toothpick. Combine the oil, lemon juice, salt and pepper. Place the stuffed squid in the marinade and let sit for 1 hour in the fridge. Next, grill the squid over medium heat, or sear for 2 minutes on each side in a preheated skillet. After cooking, deglaze with the marinade and serve these steaming and extraordinary squid immediately!

Marinated Mushrooms
à l'italienne

2 cups (250 g)	**Mushrooms, halved**
¼ cup (60 mL)	**Anchoyade oil**
¼ cup (60 mL)	**Balsamic vinegar**
1	**Garlic clove, finely chopped**
¼ cup (30 g)	**Italian parsley, chopped**
To taste	**Salt and ground pepper**

*I*n a skillet, sauté the mushrooms in anchoyade oil for 1 minute over high heat. Deglaze with the balsamic vinegar, and reduce by half (approximately 2 minutes). Place the mushrooms in a large salad bowl, and incorporate the garlic and parsley. Combine, and marinate for approximately 1 hour in the fridge. Serve this flavored fricassee that passes for an antipasto with squid or with any other southern European dish.

Pork Chops

à la portugaise

¼ cup (60 mL)	**Anchoyade oil**
1	**Small onion, chopped**
2	**Garlic cloves, chopped**
3	**Anchovy fillets, diced**
½ cup (125 g)	**Mushrooms, chopped**
6	**Sun-dried tomatoes, chopped**
4 x 5 oz (150 g)	**Pork chops**
1	**Shallot, chopped**
2 tbsp (20 g)	**Flour**
¼ cup (60 mL)	**Port**
1 cup (250 mL)	**Veal stock or beef stock**

*F*irst, prepare the stuffing. In 2 tbsp (30 mL) of anchoyade oil, brown the onion, garlic, anchovies, mushrooms and sun-dried tomatoes for about 2 minutes, stirring constantly. Let cool.

As the stuffing cools, make a fine cut into each chop, using a knife.

Then, insert the stuffing, using a pastry bag or a spoon. Pour the remaining oil into the skillet and sear the chops over high heat for 1 minute on each side. Preheat the oven to 350°F (180°C) and finish cooking for 10 minutes.

To prepare the sauce, use the same pan that was used to cook the chops and sweat the shallot. Dust with flour, stirring constantly. Cook for 1 minute, then deglaze, using the port. Moisten with the stock, and reduce for at least 5 minutes over medium heat.

Cover each chop with the well-rounded and sweet port sauce.

Anchoyade

Spaghetti

1 lb (450 g)	**Spaghetti**
¼ cup (60 mL)	**Anchoyade oil**
2	**Garlic cloves, finely chopped**
2	**Onions, diced**
1 dozen	**Garlic olives, pitted and halved**
8	**Plum tomatoes, halved**
2 tbsp (10 g)	**Fresh Italian parsley, chopped**
1 tin (48 g)	**Anchovy fillets, drained, rinsed and diced**
To taste	**Salt and ground pepper**
2 tbsp (10 g)	**Fresh basil, chopped**
4 tbsp (60 g)	**Parmesan, freshly grated**

Cook the pasta *al dente*. As the pasta cooks, sauté and brown the garlic and onions in the anchoyade oil. Next, add the olives, tomatoes, parsley and anchovies. Season moderately with salt and pepper. Cook for 5 minutes over medium heat, until the tomatoes soften.

Drain the pasta, then pour it into a large serving bowl. Sprinkle with the anchoyade oil as desired. Incorporate the fresh basil and Parmesan cheese. Add the steaming preparation of tomatoes, mix and serve hot.

And there you have quick pasta that will seduce you by its character, freshness and ardor...

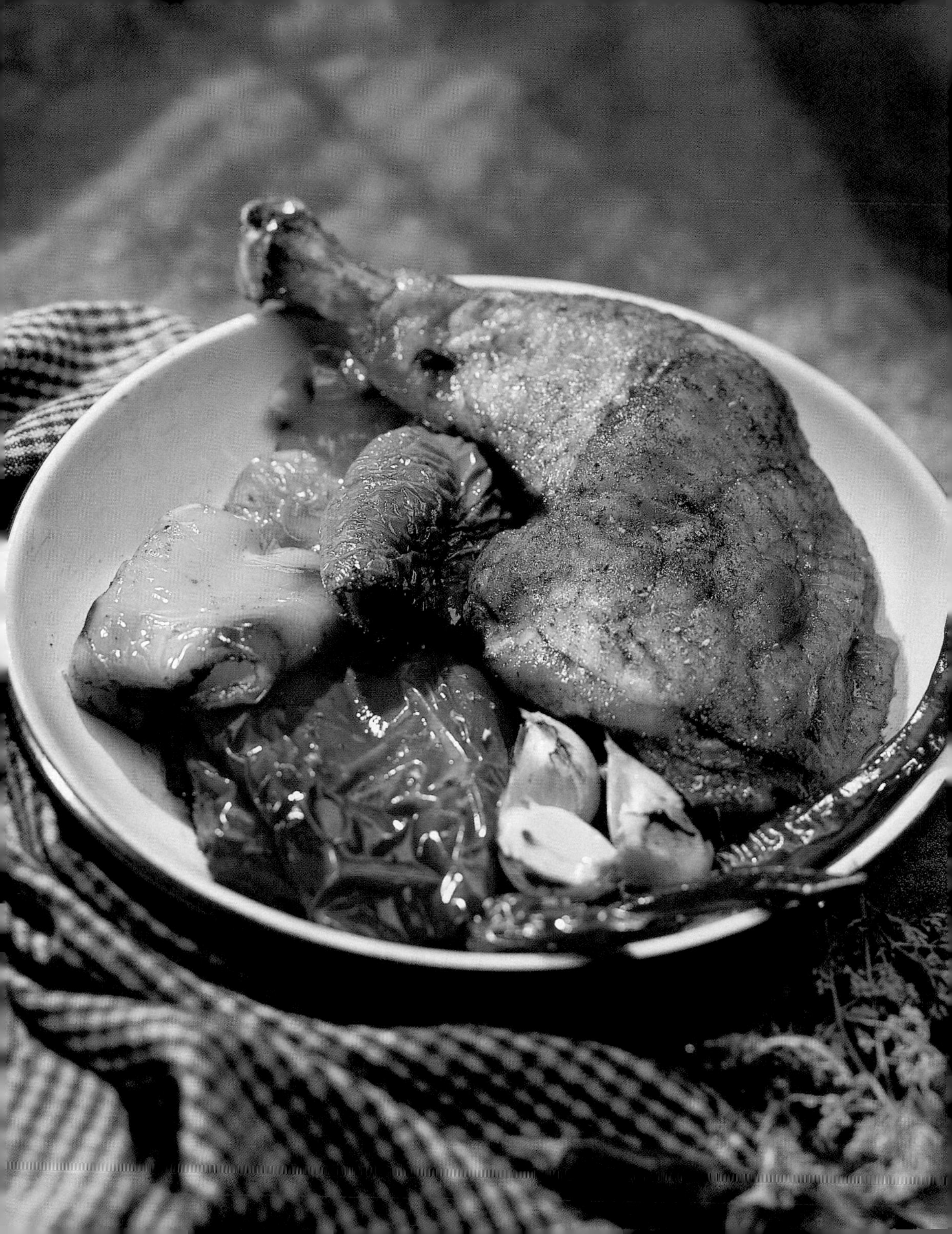

Tex-Mex
Chicken Thighs

4 x 5 oz (150 g)	**Chicken thighs**
1	**Garlic clove**
¼ cup (60 g)	**Tomato paste**
¼ cup (60 mL)	**Tex-Mex oil**
¼ cup (60 mL)	**Soya sauce or tamari**
1	**Lime (juice)**
1 tbsp (10 g)	**Paprika**
1 tbsp (15 g)	**Coriander seeds, coarsely crushed**
To taste	**Salt and ground pepper**

*T*rim the chicken thighs and rub with the garlic clove.

Thoroughly combine the tomato paste, Tex-Mex oil, soya sauce and lime juice. Brush the chicken thighs with this preparation, then sprinkle with paprika and coriander. Season with salt and pepper.

Preheat the oven to 350°F (180°C). Arrange the chicken thighs on a baking sheet and bake for 20 to 30 minutes, or grill them on the barbecue. Brown and baste several times with the Tex-Mex oil.

Serve the crispy, spicy thighs on a bed of grilled peppers...A small explosive recipe that will ignite the taste buds of your guests!

Tuna Steaks

with Fruit Salsa

$^1/_4$ cup (60 ml)	**Tex-Mex oil**
2	**Limes (juice)**
To taste	**Salt and ground pepper**
4 x 5 oz (150 g)	**Fresh tuna**
1	**Red onion, diced**
2	**Green onions, chopped**
1	**Garlic clove, chopped**
1	**Green pepper, diced**
1	**Yellow pepper, diced**
1	**Red pepper, diced**
1	**Pear, diced**
1	**Fresh mango, diced**
To taste	**Fresh coriander**

*P*repare a marinade using the Tex-Mex oil, lime juice, salt and pepper. Place the tuna in the marinade and let sit for at least 1 hour in the fridge.

During this time, prepare the salsa. Brown the onions and garlic in 2 tbsp of Tex-Mex oil. Then, add the diced peppers, pear and mango. Deglaze with the juice of the second lime and remove from heat. Sprinkle with the fresh coriander and season with salt and pepper.

Grill or fry the tuna, as desired, for 1 to 2 minutes on each side, until the fish is well grilled on the outside and still pink on the inside.

Arrange each slice on a portion of salsa and trickle warm marinade over top.

Pork Brochettes
with Santa Fe Peanuts

$^1/4$ cup (60 mL)	**Tex-Mex oil**
2 tbsp (30 mL)	**Honey**
2 tbsp (30 mL)	**Soya sauce or tamari**
1	**Lime (juice)**
2	**Garlic cloves, chopped**
To taste	**Salt and ground pepper**
8 x 5 oz (150 g)	**Pork strips (cut into 2 fillets)**
$^1/2$ cup (125 g)	**Peanuts, chopped**

Prepare the marinade by completely combining the oil, honey, soya sauce, lime juice, garlic, salt and pepper.

Make the brochettes using the pork strips and marinate overnight.

Grill or fry the brochettes for 2 to 3 minutes per side. Sprinkle with the coarsely chopped peanuts.

Serve immediately on vegetable chow mein cooked *al dente* and let yourself be carried away by the contrasts in taste and flavors that playfully alternate between spicy and sweet.

Truffle-Flavored
Beef Filet Mignon

$^{1}/4$ cup (60 mL)	**Truffle oil**
$^{1}/4$ cup (60 mL)	**Red wine**
2	**Garlic cloves, minced**
1	**Pinch of salt**
1 tsp (5 g)	**Crushed pepper**
1 tbsp (5 g)	**Fresh rosemary**
4 x 5 oz (150 g)	**Filet mignon**
1 cup (250 mL)	**Beef stock**

First, prepare the marinade by thoroughly combining the truffle oil, red wine, garlic, salt and pepper.

Place the filet mignon in the marinade and let sit in the fridge for about half a day.

In a frying pan or on the grill, sear the meat and cook as desired. Keep warm in the oven, preheated to 400°F (200°C).

Deglaze the pan with the marinade, and moisten immediately with the beef stock. Reduce by half.

Slice the filets mignons into escalopes and cover with the steaming cooking juice. Serve with mashed potatoes and truffles, on special occasions, and with butter on other days . . . unless you deserve the opposite!

Warm Chicken Liver Salad
with Truffles and Vinegar

4	**Slices of smoked bacon, diced**
4 tbsp (60 mL)	**Truffle oil**
1	**Pinch of sugar**
1 lb (450 g)	**Chicken livers**
To taste	**Salt and ground pepper**
4 tbsp (60 mL)	**Red wine vinegar**
10 oz (300 g)	**Mixed salad**
3	**Shallots, minced**
1 dozen	**Garlic croutons**

*I*n a frying pan, cook the bacon over high heat until golden brown. Add the truffle oil and sugar. Sauté the chicken livers for 2 to 4 minutes, depending on their size (they must be pink inside). Deglaze with the red wine vinegar, and pour this steaming preparation over the nest of greens in a large salad bowl.

Garnish with the minced shallots and garlic croutons. Serve warm.

Omelette
with Black Truffles

8	**Large, whole eggs**
2 tsp (10 g)	**Fresh chives**
To taste	**Salt and ground pepper**
1	**Large onion, finely chopped**
2 tbsp (30 mL)	**Truffle oil**
2	**Fresh tomatoes, cut into quarters**
1	**Truffle, finely sliced**

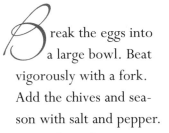

Break the eggs into a large bowl. Beat vigorously with a fork. Add the chives and season with salt and pepper.

In a large frying pan, brown the onion in the truffle oil. Add the tomato quarters, then the sliced truffle, and immediately incorporate the eggs. Cook over medium heat for 2 minutes, stirring frequently toward the center. Cover and cook over low heat for 2 to 4 minutes. Serve the omelette runny, or as you like, in a large uncovered serving dish and garnish with fresh chives. Here is a lunch fit for a king or a queen, and you undoubtedly deserve it!

Shrimp and Pasta Salad
with Saffron Oil

12	**Asparagus spears, blanched**
4 cups (640 g)	**Fusilli cooked *al dente***
1	**Fresh tomato, diced**
1	**Leek, blanched and minced**
12	**Large shrimp, cooked and shelled**
1	**Lemon (juice and zest)**
1 cup (250 mL)	**Saffron mayonnaise (see page 205)**
To taste	**Salt and ground pepper**
1	**Pinch of saffron**

Mince the blanched asparagus, setting the tips aside.

In a large salad bowl, incorporate the pasta, asparagus stems, diced tomato, minced leek, shrimp, lemon juice and saffron mayonnaise. Combine and season to taste with salt and pepper. Garnish with the asparagus tips and a pinch of saffron.

Serve cold and decorate with the lemon zest.

Saffron

Seviche

1 lb (450 g)	Large, fresh scallops, halved
$^1/_2$	Red bell pepper
1	Shallot, finely chopped
2 tbsp (20 g)	Fresh coriander, finely chopped
1 tsp (3 g)	Saffron
$^1/_4$ cup (60 mL)	Saffron oil
2	Limes (juice)
To taste	Salt and ground pepper

Incorporate all the ingredients in a large bowl, then let sit in the fridge for 1 hour. Serve very fresh, garnishing with a slice of lime and a few fresh coriander leaves.

Until proven otherwise, this is the best way to appreciate fresh scallops—the only way to taste the sea...and to enjoy the world...

Risotto

à la milanaise

¹/4 cup (60 mL)	**Saffron oil**
1	**Small onion, finely chopped**
1	**Garlic clove, finely chopped**
1 ³/4 cups (300 g)	**Italian arborio rice**
¹/2 cup (125 mL)	**Dry white wine**
4 cups (1 L)	**Chicken stock**
3 dozen	**Mussels**
1 tsp (3 g)	**Saffron**
¹/4 cup (60 mL)	**35% cream**
¹/3 cup (approx. 70 g)	**Parmesan, freshly grated**
To taste	**Ground pepper**

*H*eat 2 tbsp of saffron oil in a saucepan, brown and sweat the onions and garlic. Add the rice, then moisten with the white wine and chicken stock. Cover and simmer over low heat for 15 minutes, stirring frequently.

Next, incorporate the fresh mussels and saffron. Cover again and cook for an additional 5 minutes, stirring again and again . . .

Once the mussels have opened, add the remaining oil, cream and Parmesan. Mix, and sprinkle with freshly ground pepper.

Serve immediately accompanied by a bowl of grated Parmesan.

You will understand why Italian cooking is considered one of the best in the world . . . The best, as the Italians themselves will proudly tell you!

95

Rigatoni

with Porcini Mushrooms, Rosa Sauce

1 lb (500 g)	**Rigatoni, cooked**
3	**Shallots, minced**
1/4 cup (60 mL)	**Porcini mushroom oil**
1/2 cup (125 g)	**Rehydrated porcini mushrooms**
1/4 cup (60 mL)	**35% cream**
2	**Fresh tomatoes, diced**
2 tbsp (20 g)	**Dried thyme**
To taste	**Salt and ground pepper**

Cook the pasta *al dente*. First, sauté the shallots in the oil and cook until golden brown. Add the porcini mushrooms to the oil and cook for a few minutes, then add the cream.

Reduce by half and add the tomatoes, shallots, thyme, salt and pepper. Reduce again. Add this creamy pink sauce to the warm pasta. Garnish with a few sprigs of fresh thyme and savor without restraint . . .

Veal Escalopes

with a Cheese-Mushroom Duo

8	**Slices of portobello mushroom**
2 tbsp (30 g)	**Butter**
8	**Fontina or mozzarella cheese sticks**
8	**Veal escalopes, very thin**
4 tbsp (60 g)	**Flour**
To taste	**Salt and ground pepper**
$^1/_4$ cup (60 mL)	**Porcini mushroom oil**
$^1/_4$ cup (60 mL)	**White wine**
$^1/_4$ cup (60 mL)	**35% cream**

First, sauté the portobello mushroom slices in the butter. Arrange one slice of portobello mushroom and one cheese stick side by side on each veal escalope. Roll them up, and close using a toothpick. Flour and season with salt and pepper.

Grill on all sides in the oil for 5 minutes over medium heat. Remove and keep warm.

Deglaze the pan with the white wine. Add the cream, salt and pepper. Reduce by half. When ready to serve, cover each escalope with the tasty and rich cream sauce.

Chicken and
Mushroom Panini

1	**Red bell pepper, minced**
1/4 cup (60 mL)	**Porcini mushroom oil**
1 lb (500 g)	**White mushrooms, minced**
1 lb (500 g)	**Portobello mushrooms, sliced**
To taste	**Salt and ground pepper**
4	**Chicken breasts, cut into strips**
1	**Baguette, cut in quarters**
2 cups (500 g)	**Mozzarella, grated**

Sauté the pepper at high heat in the porcini oil. Next, add the minced white mushrooms and the portobello mushroom slices. Sauté over high heat for 3 minutes. Season with salt and pepper. Then, add the chicken breasts to this vegetable fricassee. Grill for 3 minutes on each side. Divide this preparation into 4 portions and spread on the 4 sections of baguette, on which porcini oil has already been brushed. Then, lay the mozzarella on top.

Close and place the sandwiches in a panini oven or, if you do not have one, heat them, pressing on them, in a non-stick skillet for 2 minutes on each side, until the bread is grilled and the mozzarella melted and runny . . .

Pork Paillards

with Fines herbes

1 tbsp (10 g)	**Herbes de Provence**
1/3 cup (80 mL)	***Fines herbes* and shallot oil**
3	**Garlic cloves, finely chopped**
1	**Lemon (juice)**
To taste	**Salt and ground pepper**
2	**Shallots, finely chopped**
8	**Lean pork chops**

Prepare the marinade by thoroughly combining all the ingredients, except the pork. Flatten the pork chops with a meat mallet to make thin escalopes. Brush generously with the marinade and stack in a pile. Tightly wrap in plastic film. Marinate in the fridge overnight. Grill over high heat on the barbecue or in a frying pan for about 1 minute on each side. Serve these tender Provence-inspired and savory pork paillards immediately.

Chicken Breasts

with Parma Ham

$^1/4$ cup (60 mL)	*Fines herbes* and shallot oil
1 tbsp (10 g)	*Herbes de Provence*
4 tbsp (60 mL)	Dijon mustard
1	Lemon (juice)
To taste	Salt and ground pepper
4	Chicken breasts
4	Slices of Gruyère
8	Slices of Parma ham
8	Basil leaves

*P*repare the marinade by combining the oil, *herbes de Provence*, Dijon mustard, lemon juice, salt and pepper. Place the chicken breasts in the marinade and let sit for 2 hours in the fridge.

Next, using a paring knife, make a deep cut into each breast and fill with 1 slice of Gruyère, 2 slices of Parma ham and 2 fresh basil leaves.

Sear each breast on the barbecue or in a frying pan over high heat, for at least 5 minutes on each side. When ready to serve, slice them into escalopes to reveal the ham and melting cheese.

Crispy Pork Medallions

with Fines herbes

2	**Pork tenderloins, sliced**
To taste	**Salt and ground pepper**
$^1/_4$ cup (60 mL)	***Fines herbes* and shallot oil**
4 tbsp (60 mL)	**Dijon mustard**
1 tbsp (10 g)	***Herbes de Provence***
$^1/_4$ cup (60 g)	**Homemade bread-crumbs**
1	**Shallot, minced**

Flatten each slice of pork tenderloin to form a medallion. Season with salt and pepper. Let sit for 1 or 2 hours in the oil and mustard. Remove the pork medallions from the marinade, add the remaining ingredients to the marinade and mix, using a fork. In a preheated and oiled frying pan, sear the pork medallions for 1 minute maximum. Set aside and generously brush with breadcrumbs. Bake in the oven at 400°F (200°C) for 5 minutes, until the herb breading becomes crispy. Serve with a little pepper mayonnaise.

Oriental-Flavored
Chicken Thighs

1 tbsp (15 mL)	**Dijon mustard**
1/2 cup (125 mL)	**Soya sauce or tamari**
1 tbsp (5 g)	**Fresh ginger, grated**
2	**Limes (juice and zest)**
1/4 cup (60 mL)	**Oriental-flavored oil**
1/4 cup (60 mL)	**Sesame oil**
2	**Garlic cloves, crushed**
4	**Chicken thighs**
To taste	**Salt and ground pepper**

First, prepare the marinade by thoroughly combining all the ingredients (except the chicken), using a whisk. Season the thighs to taste with salt and pepper. Arrange them in a large bowl and cover with the marinade. Let sit overnight in the fridge.

Sear the chicken pieces in a frying pan over high heat for 2 minutes on each side. Finish cooking in the oven at 350°F (180°C) for about 20 minutes. Serve hot. You will succumb to the flavors and charms of the Orient.

Grilled Scallops

with Coconut Milk

¹/4 cup (60 mL)	**Oriental-flavored oil**
1	**Lime (juice and zest)**
1 tsp (3 g)	**Crushed chili**
1 tbsp (10 g)	**Red curry powder**
4	**Garlic cloves, finely chopped**
24	**Large scallops**
¹/2 cup (125 mL)	**Coconut milk**

*P*repare the marinade by thoroughly combining all the ingredients except the scallops and the coconut milk. Place the fresh scallops in the marinade. Let sit for 1 hour in the fridge.

In a frying pan, brown the scallops over medium heat for 2 minutes on each side. During this time, in a small, thick-bottomed saucepan, combine the marinade with the coconut milk and reduce. Serve the fried scallops covered with the sweet sauce, seasoned and flavored with the coconut milk... A fiery delight!

Pork Ribs
à l'orientale

1 1/2 lbs (750 g)	Pork ribs
4 cups (1 L)	Chicken stock
2 tbsp (30 mL)	Tomato paste
1/4 cup (60 mL)	Oriental-flavored oil
1/4 cup (60 mL)	Soya sauce or tamari
2 tbsp (30 mL)	Honey
3 tbsp (45 g)	Sesame seeds
4	Garlic cloves, crushed
4	Green onions, minced
A few drops	Tabasco sauce

Separate the pork ribs. Boil in the chicken stock for approximately 30 minutes over medium heat. During this time, thoroughly combine all the ingredients for the marinade. Set aside in the fridge. Drain the pork ribs, then let them dry for a few minutes.

Generously brush the ribs with the marinade, and grill on the barbecue or in the oven on a cookie sheet, 5 minutes on each side, until they are crispy and golden brown. Result? Spellbinding pork ribs.

Fusilli with
Salmon and Red Pepper

4 cups (500 g)	**Fusilli**
1	**Red bell pepper, finely chopped**
2	**Shallots, finely chopped**
$^1/_4$ cup (60 mL)	**Pepper oil**
1 dozen	**Black Kalamata olives, pitted and minced**
7 oz (200 g)	**Cooked or canned salmon**
1	**Lemon (juice and zest)**
$^1/_4$ cup (60 mL)	**10% or 35% cream**
To taste	**Salt and ground pepper**
1	**Ripe avocado, diced**
As needed	**Parmesan, grated**

Cook the fusilli *al dente*. As the fusilli cooks, prepare the sauce. In a small saucepan, heat and brown the peppers and shallots in 2 tbsp (30 mL) of pepper oil. Add the olives, salmon, lemon juice and zest, then the cream. Heat over low heat for a few minutes, stirring regularly with a wooden spoon. Add the diced avocado at the last minute and heat for another few seconds. Drain the pasta and add the remaining oil. Pour into a large serving dish and cover with the steaming sauce. Garnish with a little Parmesan, as needed.

Here is a quick pasta dish that will thrill you ... An everyday dish that is easily prepared, even on special days!

Fresh Mussel Salad

with Peppers and Green Onions

4 dozen	**Fresh mussels**
$^1/4$ cup (60 mL)	**Dry white wine**
6	**Green onions, minced**
1	**Bunch of Italian parsley, finely chopped**
$^1/4$ cup (60 mL)	**Pepper oil**
1	**Red bell pepper, finely chopped**
$^1/4$ cup (60 mL)	**Garlic and basil vinegar**
To taste	**Salt and ground pepper**

Scrape and clean the mussels. In a large saucepan, bring the white wine, green onions and half the parsley to a boil. Add the mussels and cover. Boil for about 5 minutes, or until all the shells have opened. Discard any closed mussels. Chill. Keep the cooking juice, heat and reduce by half.

Prepare the marinade, using a whisk to thoroughly combine the oil, red pepper, vinegar, remaining parsley, reduced cooking juice, salt and pepper. Shell the mussels, keeping one half of each shell. Combine the mussels with the marinade and let sit in the fridge overnight. Serve cold in the half-shells.

Plump, tender and slightly orange in color, the marinated mussels will melt in your mouth, leaving pearls of flavor . . .

Veal Shank
with Peppers

1	**Red bell pepper, diced**
3	**Garlic cloves, minced**
1	**Small onion, finely chopped**
3	**Shallots, minced**
$^{1}/_{4}$ cup (60 mL)	**Pepper oil**
2 tbsp (30 g)	**Flour**
6 to 8	**Veal shanks**
$^{1}/_{4}$ cup (60 mL)	**White wine**
2 cups (500 mL)	**Chicken stock**
1	**Large can of tomatoes**
1 tsp (3 g)	**Thyme**
1 tsp (3 g)	**Rosemary**
To taste	**Salt and ground pepper**

*B*rown and sweat the peppers, garlic, onion and shallots in half the pepper oil over medium heat. Coat the bottom of an oven-proof casserole dish with this vegetable fricassee. Set aside. Lightly flour the veal shanks. Brown all sides in the remaining oil over medium heat. Next, arrange them in the casserole dish.

Deglaze the frying pan immediately with the white wine. Moisten with the chicken stock and reduce by half. Add the tomatoes and reduce again. Cover the shanks with this sauce. Season with the thyme, rosemary, salt and pepper. Cover and bake in the oven at 300°F (125°C) for at least 3 hours, until the veal becomes tender and the aroma of this dish envelops the house.

Delizioso!

Tagliatelle Salad
with Tomato Coulis

4 cups (500 g)	**Tagliatelle**
$^1/_4$ cup (60 mL)	**Pomodoro oil**
2	**Garlic cloves, minced**
1	**Can of whole tomatoes**
8	**Fresh basil leaves**
To taste	**Salt and ground pepper**
$^1/_4$ cup (60 mL)	**Balsamic vinegar**
6	**Green onions, minced**
$^1/_2$ cup (125 g)	**Feta cheese, crumbled**

Cook the pasta *al dente*. Rinse, then pour into a bowl and add 2 tbsp (30 mL) of Pomodoro oil, gently stirring with a fork. Chill. During this time, brown the garlic in the remaining oil, then add the well-drained, whole tomatoes. Season to taste with salt and pepper. Add the basil. Grill for a few minutes and deglaze with the balsamic vinegar. To produce a coulis, combine everything in the blender. Let cool. Incorporate this fresh coulis into the pasta without forgetting the minced onions and crumbled feta cheese.

Prepared quickly and simply, this delicious and colorful fresh pasta salad will surprise you with its character and spirit.

Grilled Snapper Fillets

with Dried Tomatoes

$^1/4$ cup (60 mL)	**Pomodoro oil**
1	**Lemon (juice and zest)**
1 tbsp (10 g)	**Dried oregano**
2	**Green onions, minced**
To taste	**Salt and ground pepper**
4	**Snapper fillets**
2 tbsp (30 g)	**Sun-dried tomatoes, minced**

*P*repare the marinade by combining the oil, lemon juice and zest, oregano, green onions, salt and pepper. Marinate the fish for 30 minutes in the fridge.

Grill the fillets on the barbecue or in a frying pan for 5 minutes, skin-side down. Deglaze with the marinade at the last moment and arrange the flavored fish on a nest of crispy greens. Garnish with the minced sun-dried tomatoes.

This simple and subtly flavored marinade will gently highlight the delicate taste of the snapper.

Grilled Eggplant and Fresh Tomato Salad

with Bocconcini

$1/3$ cup (80 mL)	**Pomodoro oil**
$1/4$ cup (60 mL)	**Balsamic vinegar**
6	**Basil leaves, minced**
To taste	**Salt and pepper**
4	**Bocconcini balls, finely sliced**
1	**Small eggplant, sliced thinly**

First, prepare the marinade by thoroughly combining the oil, vinegar, basil, salt and pepper. Marinate the bocconcini and eggplant slices in this marinade for 1 hour in the fridge.

In a preheated and oiled frying pan, grill and brown the eggplant slices and set aside. On a large serving dish, alternately arrange a slice of bocconcini, a slice of tomato and a slice of eggplant, and so on. Cover this antipasto with the remaining marinade. Season to taste with salt and pepper. This very simple antipasto promises to be a culinary delight.

Vinegars

Vinegars

Production,
Storage and
Practical Advice

Spontaneously and accidentally discovered, vinegar is a kind of offspring of wine, destined for a new world of fabulous tastes, flavors and aromas.

Powerful and exuberant, vinegar clearly asserts its character by making its mark in the kitchen. Discover the different types and different uses. By way of images, words, recipes and advice, I invite you to meet this ally!

A little history   As is true of many of humankind's discoveries, vinegar was stumbled upon by chance. Spontaneously created when wine was fermented for a second time, vinegar is closely related to wine itself, and goes back to Gallo-Roman times: a long, long time ago, uncorked wine left exposed to air and heat is

believed to have produced a marvelous vinegar. From then on, wine would be deliberately left exposed to produce a few liters of acrid wine, an astringent beverage that was diluted with a little water and drunk quickly, a precious liquor to which therapeutic benefits were attributed. The Roman legionnaires were crazy about it! From here, it is not much of a leap to believing that vinegar was the secret to the strength of this famous army.

Vinegar was thus produced for thousands of years without an understanding of the principles of fermentation. It took Pasteur sticking his nose into this bitter preparation to understand that vinegar is caused by a microorganism that is naturally present in air, a microorganism called *mycoderma aceti*. It is this famous bacterium that gradually forms a creamy, viscous gray veil on the surface of wine, which thickens, then ripples, and gradually descends into the liquid, transforming the alcohol into acetic acid. Colloquially, *mycoderma aceti* is known as "vinegar mother" or, even better, as the Italians say, *mamma . . .*

Production

Bittersweetness borne by mother . . . The great vinegars are derived from alcohol and "vinegar mother." Whether they are made from wine, cider, malt or rice alcohol, the method remains the same. This round and bitter liquid comes from the *mamma*. Acetification of the alcohol occurs when it comes in contact with air. Once the vinegar mother has formed on the surface of the liquid, it is left to float, partially uncovered, for a month or two in a wooden barrel, glass container or stoneware vinegar bottle. The wine alcohol is thus transformed into acetic acid. Depending on the method, the producer and the know-how, the vinegar is aged in oak barrels for several months, or even, as in the case of balsamic or sherry vinegars, several years. The longer the vinegar is left to age in the barrel, the rounder, more delectable and tasty it is, and the less acidic and harsh it seems to be. This is, therefore, a simple and natural method that is used to prepare artisanal vinegar. Time passes slowly, as the good wine ferments and the vinegar evolves and improves. Next, it is harvested and, especially, savored and enjoyed...

Bitterness borne
by industry . . .

Commercially produced vinegars have little in common with the artisanal type; they are made as quickly as possible, impatiently and without much respect for the *mamma*, the finished product or the food lover. The vinegar is produced in immense stainless steel vats, often within less than a day, from white wine, red wine, cider or any other type of alcohol, stirred and blended hot with beechwood chips sprayed with vinegar, or even bacteria. The insignificant biting vinegar that is thus obtained is then pasteurized and sometimes distilled before being bottled... and finally consumed without a great deal of pleasure.

Does vinegar appeal to you? Why not prepare it yourself, in your own way, according to your own taste? Nothing could be simpler. In a glass or

Make it yourself!

stoneware container, in a small oak barrel or, even better, in a real vinegar bottle, pour in a good-quality white or red wine, or any other type of alcohol of your choice, and place a piece of vinegar mother on top. Plug the opening with a cloth or a perforated cover to allow air to pass through and to enable the poor little "mother" to breathe a little; deprived of air, she could suffocate, waste away, even die. Let sit at room temperature for a month or two and the wine will become magnificently sour. Add the remaining wine or fruit and create your own aromatic combinations. Each quantity of vinegar removed should immediately be replaced with the equivalent amount of wine.

If you do not have any vinegar mother, all you have to do is combine, in equal proportions, alcohol (red or white wine, cider, sherry, etc.) and vinegar. Fermentation will occur spontaneously, but the transformation to vinegar will take longer. It will not be ready to use for two or three months.

Buying Vinegar

Lacking in charm and bouquet, the only vinegar available for a long time was the sad industrial white spirit vinegar, a corrosive, abrasive acetic acid of little interest. Fortunately, it is now possible to find the impossible when it comes to vinegar. Dozens of varieties of color, taste and price have begun to appear on the shelves of grocery stores and specialty shops. How to choose, how to buy from such a vast selection? Without doubt, artisanal vinegar is preferable to industrial vinegar, unless, of course, you are using it to clean your tiles or your boots in winter. For cooking, artisanal vinegar, well-rounded, will become a veritable ally and reveal a bouquet of surprising flavors. Its acid taste will be warm and enveloping, rather than abrasive and harsh. The large difference in price will seem justified.

Do not hesitate to buy vinegar with vinegar mother deposits in it; these deposits are a clear indication that the vinegar is artisanal. They also testify to the quality of the vinegar and assert its vitality. Discover and explore the possibilities of each type of vinegar, whether natural or flavored, each one with its own particular taste. The quality of a vinegar is determined not only by how it is made, but, even more so, by the quality of alcohol from which it is made : a vinegar will never be better than the wine from which it comes.

Storage

Vinegar is a natural and fearlessly efficient preservative used in the preparation of numerous marinades. Clearly, then, it is far from being capricious and fragile, and, unlike oil, requires little care. The pantry remains the best storage place. Protected from heat and light, vinegar will keep for several years. It is possible that, with time, it will lose its color, but even then it is as lively and high-spirited as ever. In unpasteurized vinegars, small gelatinous deposits or threads will inevitably develop. Not to worry : it is only the vinegar mother quietly appearing. This deposit is edible; however, if this "maternal" presence bothers you, simply

filter the vinegar through a fine sieve or, even better, use it to add to wine to prepare your own vinegar. Should the vinegar become cloudy and lose its transparency, it would be better to discard it to avoid any gastric problems. Aside from this unlikely decline, the vinegar will stay well-rounded, tenacious and lively for a very long time.

Use

If, until now, you have only used vinegar as an ingredient in your vinaigrettes and salad dressings, then I invite you to try something original and daring by using this bitter liquid differently. If used wisely and in measured amounts, vinegar can give your cooking both body and tone. Use it naturally or flavored, combined with a little oil and aromatics, tomato sauce, honey or fruit juice, to marinate your meats. In contact with this acid, meat becomes tender and more flavorful. Prepare warm salads by deglazing offal and poultry with red wine vinegar or a well-rounded balsamic vinegar.

Next, arrange this warm and scented meat on a bed of crunchy greens. Season your cream sauces with a few drops of bitter vinegar. They will magically sweeten and become even creamier. Use cider or malt vinegar to season chutneys, ketchups and court bouillons. Use it to preserve all the freshness of the vegetables included in your marinades.

And white vinegar? Ah, yes! The sad white vinegar. Well, sprinkle it on your fries! For this, I agree, it is still perfectly suited.

The World
of Vinegar

*C*ould it be that you still mourn the time when white vinegar was king and our cooking boring and colorless? Are you at a loss when confronted with the alarming choice of lesser and greater vintages? Let me guide and advise you. What follows is a profile of these bittersweet companions, generous with their flavors, unequivocal, full of brio and energy. Time to discover!

Balsamic Vinegar

This is truly nectar, a magnificent vinegar. Balsamic is an *appellation contrôlée* vinegar. Exceptional, this vinegar originates from Modena, a city in northern Italy. It is a delight that has been produced for centuries with love and know-how, according to a complex recipe.

Balsamic vinegar is made from the sweet grape must of the white Trebbiano Ugni Blanc that is harvested late in the fall to allow it to soak up sunshine and develop flavor. At the first sign that the must is fermenting, it is heated and reduced by approximately $3/4$ to concentrate the taste, perfumes and aromas. The resulting dense, caramelized, amber-colored and syrupy juice is stored in

oak barrels until its natural and spontaneous transformation into vinegar. It is then aged in a succession of barrels made from different woods, such as chestnut, cherry, ash and finally mulberry. After being transferred from one barrel to another, it is bottled, often after many years. For vinegar to be considered balsamic, it must have spent at least four good years in barrels before it is bottled.

Use

Balsamic vinegar will add brilliance and roundness to your salads, marinades and vinaigrettes, but it would be disappointing just to use it in simple recipes. The Italians enjoy its rounded, sweet flavor over ice, drunk as an aperitif. Use this nectar to deglaze chicken and calves livers for your warm salads. Marinate meat and vegetables in this sweet, old vinegar. A few drops are enough to add roundness to sauces. Sweet and caramelized, it can happily

flavor your desserts: simply add a hint to your vanilla *gelati* and sprinkle over your fresh strawberries. *Delizioso!*

Virtues

Balsamic vinegar, just like other vinegars, stimulates the appetite and aids digestion.

Storage

Balsamic vinegar that is already relatively aged responds well to time and air. Only light and too much heat will spoil its vivacity. It is, therefore, preferable to store it in the cellar or the pantry. Thus protected, it will keep for several years without the slightest problem. Contrary to what you might expect, once out of its oak barrel and far from its native Italy, it does not improve with age.

Sherry Vinegar

Here is another superb vinegar, a little-known *grand cru*. An *appellation contrôlée* vinegar, sherry vinegar originates from Andalusia in Spain, or, more precisely, from Jerez de la Frontera, near Seville. This vinegar is derived from sherry, originally a Spanish wine. Produced from pre-served wine must and aged in oak barrels for several years, it has a dark color and an ample robust taste; it is very dry, with a lot of breadth.

Use

Thanks to its honest taste, robustness and roundness, it can be used in cooking, much as a good wine is used. I adore using it to marinate meat and poultry.

It is both irresistible and indispensable for deglazing grilled meat and vegetables. A few drops in a sauce, in a stock or on vegetables is enough to enhance the taste.

Virtues

Sherry vinegar, as with all the vinegars, stimulates the appetite and aids digestion.

Storage

Already fairly old, it ably resists time and air. Only light and heat will affect its vivacity. Therefore, it should be stored in the cellar or the pantry. Once protected, it will keep for several years without any problem. Even if sherry vinegar has all the qualities of a great wine, it hardly improves with age. Therefore, use it immediately. It would be both a pity and a shame not to enjoy this vinegar!

Wine Vinegar

There are dozens of wine vinegars on the market, from the best to the worst, from the most voluptuous to the harshest, from the most delirium-making to the dullest! Whether red, white or rosé, whether produced in Champagne or Châteuneuf-du-Pape, remember that it is never, ever, better than the wine from which it is made. Abandon industrial vinegars that are manufactured as quickly as possible without the least respect for either the wine or the *mamma*. Choose artisanal vinegar. Aged in barrels, it is rounder, sweeter and tastier. The older it is, the better it is and the longer it will retain its flavor.

Use

Whether made from red or white wine, this vinegar is both an extraordinary and essential condiment in cooking. What other condiment allows you to energize and mellow at the same time, by offering body and sensual delight? Its flavor will explode in your salads, vinaigrettes, marinades and mayonnaises. Use it without restraint in sauces, soups and stocks. Shamelessly mistreat it to deglaze your meats and, in small quantities, use it instead of wine as the base of your marinade; it will tenderize your meats quicker.

Virtues

Wine vinegar, as is the case with all the vinegars, stimulates the appetite and helps with digestion.

Storage

Wine vinegar ably resists exposure to both time and air. Only light and heat will affect its vivacity. Therefore, it should be stored in the cellar or the pantry. Thus protected, it can be kept for several years without any problem. Even though this vinegar is made from wine, it hardly improves with age. Therefore, use it immediately. It would be a shame to put off such pleasure! Unpasteurized vinegar may develop a slight viscous deposit with time. Fear not as it is only the deliciously edible vinegar mother. If she bothers you, filter her out, making her disappear until her next visit.

Cider Vinegar

This is a fine, sweet and fruity vinegar. Its beautiful amber color recalls that of the pure, natural apple juice which serves as its base. Aged in oak barrels for nearly one year and sometimes more, depending on the producer, artisanal cider vinegar is deliciously round and startling. Some local producers make incomparable cider vinegar that is worth as much as expensive imported wine vinegars.

Use

Each type of vinegar offers its own share of food pleasures and discoveries; it is just a question of taming the accents. Cider vinegar marvelously seasons salads and crudités, and its mildness allows it to be used in court bouillons as well as in fish and seafood dishes. Poultry is also admirably in tune with its sweet harmony. As with all the other vinegars, it is superb in marinades, for deglazing meats and for adding flavor to sauces. It is also magnificent in a salad cleverly combining fruit and vegetables.

Virtues

A large number of health virtues have been attributed to vinegar in general, and to cider vinegar in particular. It is no longer consumed solely for its taste, but increasingly for its medicinal qualities. Its use, encouraged by naturopaths, has become a veritable magic potion. Whether cheerfully used in cooking or consumed daily with a little water, as is recommended by some, cider vinegar will bring its benefits to the body. A tonic, it is invigorating and stimulating, and aids digestion. Myth or reality, alternative

and traditional medicine can debate this question without me. Whatever the scientific reality, the enjoyment obtained from consuming cider vinegar is very real and deliciously palpable.

Storage

Cider vinegar, as do all the other vinegars, survives when exposed to time and air. Only light and heat will affect its vivacity. Therefore, it should be stored in the cellar or the pantry. Protected, it will keep for several years without the slightest problem. The vinegar mother that will inevitably form in the bottom of a bottle of unpasteurized vinegar is edible. However, if it bothers you, simply filter it out.

Malt Vinegar

Mild and delicious, malt vinegar is unfortunately misunderstood and neglected. Derived from barley sprout juice and initially colorless, you will often see it amber-colored like cognac as it is sometimes tinted and flavored with a little caramel. Readily available in grocery stores in its commercial form, it is rarely found in its artisanal form.

Use

This vinegar is very good for cooking, and excellent for use in marinades and preserves. It marvelously seasons fried or grilled fish and gives fries some panache. It is also a taste ally for all your chutneys, ketchups and fruit compotes. It leaves a clear mark of its good taste sprinkled on fresh cucumber salad!

Virtues

As in the case of other vinegars, malt vinegar stimulates the appetite and helps with digestion.

Storage

Malt vinegar, as with all other vinegars, is impervious to both time and air. Light and heat will, however, affect its vivacity. It may discolor slightly with time. Have no fear as this in no way changes its properties or its taste. It is, however, recommended that it be kept in the cellar or the pantry. Thus protected, the vinegar can be kept for several years without the slightest problem. The vinegar mother that will inevitably form at the bottom of the unpasteurized vinegar bottles is edible. However, if it bothers you, simply filter it out.

Rice Vinegar

An Asian creation offering beautiful taste adventures, this vinegar is made from fermented acrid rice wine. The Japanese like it sweet, mellow and flavored, while the Chinese prefer theirs spicy, strong and bitter. Sometimes flavored and scented with ginger, chili, or even sesame, rice vinegar is just as tasty in its pure state.

Use

It is also delicious and indispensable for marinating meats and is a reliable ally for all sweet-and-sour sauces widely used in Oriental cooking. Combined with a hint of soya sauce, a glassful of sesame oil and a few drops of Tabasco sauce, it wakes up the taste of spinach and bean sprout salads and tantalizes slumbering Western taste buds!

Virtues

Rice vinegar, as do all vinegars, stimulates the appetite and aids digestion.

Storage

Rice vinegar, as do all vinegars, responds very well to both time and air. However, light and heat will affect its vivacity. It is, therefore, recommended that it be stored in the cellar or the pantry. Thus protected, the vinegar can be kept for several years without any problem.

Candied grape and tarragon vinegar

Garlic and

Balsamic vinegar with chili and jalapeño peppers

Red berry vinegar

Flavored *Vinegars*

V inegar has always proven to be an efficient preservative. It is tame and receptive to aromatics, spices, *fines herbes*, condiments and vegetables—all that come into contact with it. Vinegar effortlessly absorbs the flavors and scents that it is offered. Even if they are exuberant by nature, these bitter liquids can improve. Carefully managed, the most banal vinegar can benefit from any marriage you might propose. Go ahead, I dare you.

*Balsamic vinegar with
chili and jalapeño peppers*

Balsamic Vinegar with Chili and Jalapeño Peppers

This is a spicy and lively vinegar. Its magnificent nectar will burst in your mouth and energetically season all your sauces, marinades and grilled dishes.

2 cups (500 mL)	**Balsamic vinegar**
2 tbsp (30 g)	**Crushed chili**
2	**Jalapeño peppers, finely sliced**

Bring the balsamic vinegar to a low boil. Next, incorporate the crushed chili and the jalapeño slices. Simmer over medium heat for 3 to 5 minutes. Remove from heat and let cool. Pour the mixture into a bottle or very clean jar. Let steep in the pantry for about 2 weeks. Filter through a fine sieve. Should be used sparingly . . . this mixture is explosive!

Recipes

Veal Medallions with a Mushroom Trio

Carpaccio Duo with Balsamic Vinegar

Vegetable Fricassee with Modena Vinegar

Other suggestions

Devilled Pork Ribs

Grilled Flank with Honey and Spices

Calf's Liver and Mushrooms with Balsamic Vinegar

Exotic Fruit Vinegar

Here is a sweet, delightfully fruity vinegar, slightly syrupy and filled with sunshine. This vinegar combines the color of the Caribbean with the taste of the Tropics.

6	**Candied apricots**
2 tbsp (30 g)	**Candied papaya, diced**
2 tbsp (30 g)	**Candied pineapple, diced**
2 cups (500 mL)	**White wine vinegar**

Recipes

Parma Ham with Mango and Red Peppers

Pork Ribs with Exotic Fruit

Duck Breast with Candied Papaya

Other suggestions

Pork Loin with Rum and Pineapple

Glazed Roast Pork with Sweet and Sour Peaches

Lamb Chops with Sweet and Sour Marmalade

Place the candied fruit in a very clean bottle or jar and moisten with the white wine vinegar. Tightly seal and let steep in the pantry for 2 to 3 weeks, until the candied fruits swell, fill with vinegar, and deliciously abandon their flavors. Shake the bottle well before using, to allow the fruit syrup to diffuse in the bottle.

Red berry vinegar

Red Berry Vinegar

This is a lively, fruity and nervous vinegar ... a vinegar with red tones, blue highlights and a wild taste.

2 cups (500 mL)	**Red wine vinegar**
1 dozen	**Fresh or deep-frozen cranberries**
Approx. 20	**Gooseberries or black-berries**
Approx. 20	**Raspberries**

Bring the vinegar to a boil. Incorporate the red fruit and simmer over medium heat for 3 to 5 minutes, until all the fresh fruit has colored and flavored the vinegar. Let cool. Next, let this delicious nectar steep in a very clean bottle or a jar, sheltered from light and heat, for at least 3 weeks. Filter through a fine sieve, saving only the transparent and crystalline vinegar. You can garnish your bottle with some of the fresh cranberries.

Recipes

Rack of Lamb with Wild Berries

Calf's Liver with Red Berry Compote

Hot Chèvre with Red Berries and Spices

Other suggestions

Warm Chicken and Lardoon Salad Flavored with Red Berries

Bison Breast with Cranberry Coulis

Tomatoes Stuffed with Snow Crab, Fruit Vinegar

Garlic and Basil Vinegar

This vinegar has a lot of breadth, character and a beautiful exuberance. A vinegar with ample taste and imbued with flavors from the garden and the scent of summer.

2 cups (500 mL)	**Red wine vinegar**
6	**Garlic cloves, minced**
Approx. 20	**Large fresh basil leaves, shredded**

Recipes

Devilled Chicken Brochettes

Gazpacho Duo with Garlic and Basil

Mixed Salad with Grilled Mozzarella

Other suggestions

Celery Salad Remoulade

Warm Squid Salad with Grilled Peppers

Potato Salad with Bacon and Cheddar

First, bring the vinegar to a boil. Turn off the heat. Incorporate the garlic and fresh basil and let infuse until cool. Decant into a jar or clean bottle and let sit as is for 3 weeks, sheltered from light and heat, for example, in the pantry. Next, filter through a fine sieve, saving only the vinegar.

Candied grape and
tarragon vinegar

Candied Grape and Tarragon Vinegar

This straw-colored vinegar has a sweet, herbaceous taste. It is an all-purpose vinegar with a smooth, mellow flavor.

2 cups (500 mL)	**White wine vinegar**
6	**Sprigs of fresh tarragon**
1/4 cup (75 g)	**Golden raisins**

Incorporate all the ingredients in a very clean pretty bottle or carafe. Let steep at least 3 weeks in the pantry, until the grapes have swelled and added a well rounded flavor to the vinegar. Do not filter, as the grapes and tarragon serve as a garnish.

Recipes

Braised Rabbit with Tarragon and Mushrooms

Warm Watercress Salad with Caramelized Shallots

Grilled Sirloin Steak, Béarnaise Sauce

Other suggestions

Chicken Breasts with Olives and Tarragon Vinegar

Zucchini Salad with Almonds

Chèvre Salad

Recipes

How

to

Use

Flavored

Vinegars

By following my suggestions and adding your imagination, you have prepared vinegars that are as delicious as they are pretty. Following are a few quick and simple recipes full of taste and surprises. It is up to me to suggest them, you to use them and all of us to enjoy them!

Veal Medallions
with Three Mushrooms

4 x 5 oz (150 g)	**Veal medallions**
1 tsp (5 g)	***Herbes de Provence***
To taste	**Salt and ground pepper**
1/4 cup (60 mL)	**Olive oil**
4	**Shallots, minced**
6	**Mushrooms, halved**
4	**Oyster mushrooms, sliced**
1	**Portobello mushroom, sliced**
1/4 cup (60 mL)	**Balsamic vinegar with chili and jalapeño peppers**
2 cups (500 mL)	**Beef stock**
4	**Knobs of butter**

Sprinkle the veal medallions with the *herbes de Provence*. Season with salt and pepper. In 2 tbsp (30 mL) of olive oil, fry the meat 4 minutes per side, then set aside and keep warm in the oven at 400°F (200°C). In the same frying pan, sweat the shallots in the remaining oil. Sauté and brown the mushrooms for about 2 minutes. Deglaze with the spicy balsamic vinegar and moisten immediately with the beef stock. Reduce by half. Bind at the last minute with the knobs of butter. Cover the pink veal medallions with the mushroom-flavored sauce. If veal sometimes seems a little boring, this explosive sauce will give it a lot of character and panache.

163

Carpaccio Duo
with Balsamic Vinegar

$^1/_3$ cup (70 mL)	**Extra-virgin olive oil or *fines herbes* and shallot oil**
$^1/_4$ cup (60 mL)	**Balsamic vinegar with chili and jalapeño peppers**
To taste	**Salt and ground pepper**
6 oz (180 g)	**Salmon fillet, finely sliced**
6 oz (180 g)	**Tuna fillet, finely sliced**
1 dozen	**Small capers**
1	**Red onion, minced**

*U*sing a whisk, emulsify the olive oil and balsamic vinegar. Add the salt and pepper. Cover the fine slices of fish with this mixture. Garnish with the capers and onion slices. Serve cold.

You will thus discover the mild, smooth taste of the sea seasoned with a few drops of explosive balsamic vinegar!

Vegetable Fricassee

with Modena Vinegar

1	**Small eggplant, sliced**
2	**Zucchinis, sliced**
1	**Red bell pepper, cut into large strips**
1	**Green bell pepper, cut into large strips**
1	**Carrot, blanched and sliced into rounds**
1	**Parsnip, blanched and sliced into rounds**
$^1/_2$ cup (125 mL)	**Extra virgin olive oil or anchoyade oil**
$^1/_3$ cup (85 mL)	**Balsamic vinegar with chili and jalapeño peppers**
1 tbsp (5 g)	**Fresh thyme, finely chopped**
To taste	**Salt and ground pepper**
3 tbsp (45 g)	**Romano cheese, freshly grated**

*I*n a large salad bowl, combine all the ingredients (except the cheese) and let sit for a good $^1/_2$ hour at room temperature. Grill the vegetables on the barbecuc (in winter, broil in the oven) about 5 to 10 minutes, regularly brushing with the marinade. Serve hot and sprinkle with the Romano cheese.

Never have vegetables offered so much flavor, aroma and pleasure . . .

Braised Rabbit

with Tarragon and Mushrooms

2 cups (500 mL)	**Extra virgin olive oil or *fines herbes* and shallot oil**
1/4 cup (60 mL)	**Candied grape and tarragon vinegar**
1	**Small onion, finely chopped**
4	**Garlic cloves, minced**
To taste	**Salt and ground pepper**
2 1/2 lbs (1.3 kg)	**Rabbit, cut into pieces**
1 lb (500 g)	**Mushrooms, whole**
2 cups (500 mL)	**Veal stock or beef stock**
1	**Bunch of fresh tarragon**
2 tbsp (30 g)	**Dijon mustard**

Preheat the oven to 250°F (125°C).

Deglaze the pan with the remaining tarragon vinegar, add the mushrooms and moisten with the veal stock or beef stock. Reduce a little. Cover the rabbit with this stock and add the bunch of tarragon. Braise for 2 hours in the oven.

Remove the tender pieces of rabbit and the mushrooms. Set aside in a large serving dish. Incorporate the mustard in the steaming sauce and mix using a fork.

Cover the rabbit with this flavored sauce and serve immediately.

Tender and spicy, this small rabbit offers a few mouthfuls of the utmost pleasure.

Prepare the marinade by combining the olive oil, 2 tbsp (30 mL) of tarragon vinegar, onion, garlic, salt and pepper. Place the pieces of rabbit in the marinade and let sit for at least 12 hours in the fridge.

In a frying pan, sear the rabbit pieces on each side over high heat. Arrange them in a casserole dish and set aside.

Warm Watercress Salad
with Caramelized Shallots

4	Bunches of watercress
$^1/4$ cup (60 mL)	Citrus oil or extra virgin olive oil
1 tsp (5 g)	Sugar
6	Shallots, minced
$^1/4$ cup (60 mL)	Candied grape and tarragon vinegar
To taste	Salt and ground pepper

Set aside the carefully washed and drained watercress in a large salad bowl. Heat the oil in a frying pan. Add the sugar and shallots. Lightly brown and caramelize for 2 minutes. Deglaze with the tarragon vinegar and reduce by half. Pour this steaming preparation over the fresh watercress. Toss after having added salt and pepper.

Serve warm.

The contrasts in flavor, warmth and texture offered by this salad will surprise you...

Grilled Sirloin Steak,

Béarnaise Sauce

MARINADE

$1/3$ cup (85 mL)	**Citrus oil or extra virgin olive oil**
$1/4$ cup (60 mL)	**Candied grape and tarragon vinegar**
2 tbsp (30 g)	**Dijon mustard**
1	**Onion, finely chopped**
To taste	**Salt and ground pepper**
4 x 5 oz (150 g)	**Sirloin steaks**

BÉARNAISE SAUCE

$1/4$ cup (60 mL)	**Candied grape and tarragon vinegar**
$1/2$ tsp (2 g)	**Ground pepper**
2	**Egg yolks**
5 oz (150 g)	**Clarified butter**
To taste	**Salt and ground pepper**

*F*irst, prepare the marinade by emulsifying the oil, vinegar and mustard. Add the onion, salt and pepper. Marinate the sirloin steaks overnight in the fridge.

Prepare the béarnaise saucc. Heat the tarragon vinegar and ground pepper in a double boiler. Add the egg yolks and beat vigorously using a whisk, incorporating the clarified butter in a thin stream. Season with salt and set aside in the double boiler over low heat.

Trim the sirloin steaks, season with salt and pepper. Grill them (according to your own taste).

Serve these superb steaks covered with this delicious béarnaise sauce and garnish with a few tarragon leaves. This recipe will give you a beautiful occasion to get reacquainted with beef... Why deny yourself the pleasure!

MARINADE

$1/2$ cup (125 mL)	**Extra virgin olive oil or citrus oil**
3 tbsp (45 mL)	**Garlic and basil vinegar**
4 tbsp (60 mL)	**Tamari**
To taste	**Salt and ground pepper**
4 x 5 oz (150 g)	**Chicken breasts, cut in three lengthwise**

Devilled Chicken
Brochettes

PEACH SAUCE

1	**Red onion, finely chopped**
3	**Garlic cloves, chopped**
2 tbsp (30 mL)	**Olive oil**
2	**Red bell peppers, seeded, peeled, grilled and diced**
2	**Peaches, pitted, peeled and diced**
1 tbsp (15 g)	**Sugar**
1/2 cup (125 mL)	**Garlic and basil vinegar**
2 cups (500 mL)	**Tomato juice**
1 tsp (5 g)	**Salt**
4	**Drops of Tabasco sauce**

*C*ombine all the ingredients in the marinade. Place the chicken breasts in the marinade and let sit for 2 hours in the fridge.

During this time, prepare the peach sauce. Sweat the onion and garlic in the olive oil. Add the peppers, peaches and sugar. Caramelize over medium heat for 5 minutes. Deglaze with the garlic and basil vinegar and moisten with the tomato juice. Add the salt and the Tabasco sauce and simmer for 10 minutes. In the blender, transform this preparation into a beautiful creamy purée.

Prepare the brochettes and grill for approximately 5 minutes. Cover with the warm peach purée.

You will be seduced by the agreeable contrast of warmth and taste.

Gazpacho Duo

with Garlic and Basil

TOMATO GAZPACHO

4	**Large ripe, red tomatoes**
1	**Red onion**
1	**Garlic clove**
1	**Red bell pepper**
2 tbsp (30 mL)	**Garlic and basil vinegar**
1 cup (250 mL)	**Tomato juice**
2 tbsp (30 mL)	**Extra virgin olive oil**
4	**Drops of Tabasco sauce**
To taste	**Salt and ground pepper**

CUCUMBER GAZPACHO

2	**Cucumbers, peeled and seeded**
1	**Green bell pepper**
1	**Jalapeño pepper**
2	**Green onions, minced**
2 tbsp (30 mL)	**Garlic and basil vinegar**
2 tbsp (10 g)	**Fresh basil, shredded**
1 cup (250 mL)	**Vegetable stock**
To taste	**Salt and ground pepper**
1 cup (250 mL)	**Sour cream**
To taste	**Fresh basil leaves**

*P*repare the two gazpachos separately, yet in the same manner. In a large bowl, combine all the ingredients, finely chopped with a knife to retain their taste, aroma and texture. If time is an issue, use a food processor. Chill in the fridge. Serve the two gazpachos in the same soup dish; avoid mixing them.

Garnish with a small dab of sour cream and a fresh basil leaf. You will be charmed and moved by the spectacle!

Mixed Salad
with Grilled Mozzarella

14 oz (400 g)	Mozzarella, thickly sliced (1 inch / 2.5 cm)
2 tbsp (30 mL)	Dijon mustard
1 cup (250 mL)	Extra virgin olive oil or *fines herbes* and shallot oil
1/3 cup (80 mL)	Garlic and basil vinegar
To taste	Salt and ground pepper
5 oz (150 g)	Mixed salad

In the oven, grill the mozzarella slices for about 2 minutes on each side.

During this time, prepare the vinaigrette by vigorously emulsifying the mustard, oil, vinegar, salt and pepper. In a large salad bowl, incorporate the vinaigrette in the salad and sprinkle with the warm, grilled mozzarella slices cut into dice.

Serve while the cheese is warm and enjoy!

Parma Ham

with Mango and Red Peppers

1	Fresh mango, cut into quarters
2	Red bell peppers, peeled, seeded, grilled and cut into large strips
8	Slices of Parma ham
$^1/_4$ cup (60 mL)	Extra virgin olive oil or *fines herbes* and shallot oil
2 tbsp (30 mL)	Exotic fruit vinegar
To taste	Salt and ground pepper
1 dozen	Garlic olives

*P*lace one strip of red pepper on each mango quarter and wrap everything in a slice of Parma ham. Emulsify the olive oil, vinegar, salt and pepper. Cover with this mixture and accompany with the garlic olives.

This is a very simple and seductive antipasto that can be prepared in the blink of an eye and devoured even quicker!

Pork Ribs

with Exotic Fruit

3 lbs (1.3 kg)	**Pork ribs**
4 cups (1 L)	**Chicken stock**
$^1/_2$ cup (125 mL)	**Tomato paste**
$^1/_4$ cup (60 mL)	**Soya sauce or tamari**
4 tbsp (60 mL)	**Honey**
2	**Garlic cloves, minced**
$^1/_4$ cup (60 mL)	**Exotic fruit vinegar**
$^1/_4$ cup (60 mL)	**Pineapple juice**

*P*reheat the oven to 400°F (200°C). Boil the pork ribs for approximately 30 minutes in the chicken stock.

Remove from the water and let cool. During this time, in a large, deep bowl, thoroughly combine all the other ingredients. Place the ribs in the marinade and let sit for at least 1 hour in the fridge, stirring from time to time. Remove the ribs and roast them for 1 hour on a cookie sheet, brushing regularly with the marinade.

These tender and fruity pork ribs should be served very hot.

Duck Breast
with Candied Papaya

4 x 6 $^1/_2$ oz (200 g)	**Duck breasts**
To taste	**Salt and pepper**
4	**Shallots, minced**
1 tbsp (15 mL)	**Olive oil**
1 tbsp (15 g)	**Sugar**
$^1/_2$ cup (approx. 65 g)	**Candied papaya, diced**
$^1/_4$ cup (60 mL)	**Exotic fruit vinegar**
2 cups (500 mL)	**Veal stock or beef stock**
1 tsp (5 g)	**Ground pepper**
2 tbsp (30 mL)	**35% cream**

*P*reheat the oven to 375°F (180°C). Trim the duck breasts and season with salt and pepper by making short incisions into the fat. On the stove, sear over high heat for 2 minutes on each side. Finish cooking for 7 minutes in the oven so that they are nicely golden brown on the outside and pink on the inside.

During this time, prepare the sauce by sweating the shallots in 1 tbsp (15 mL) of olive oil. Add the sugar and half the candied papaya.

Caramelize for approximately 2 minutes. Deglaze with the exotic fruit vinegar and moisten immediately with the veal stock or beef stock. Reduce by half and strain through a sieve, saving only the stock. Add the pepper and remaining papaya and reduce over low heat for another few minutes. Bind with the cream.

Slice the pink breasts into escalopes and cover with this Caribbean-flavored sauce.

Close your eyes when tasting this dish and sense the southern breeze and wide open spaces...

Rack of Lamb
with Wild Berries

2	**Racks of lamb**
4	**Garlic cloves, halved**
To taste	**Salt and ground pepper**
2	**Sprigs of fresh thyme, chopped**
2 tbsp (30 mL)	**Citrus oil**
$^1/_2$ cup (125 mL)	**Port**
$^1/_4$ cup (60 mL)	**Maple syrup**
$^1/_4$ cup (60 mL)	**Red berry vinegar**
$^1/_2$ cup (65 g)	**Fresh blackberries**
$^1/_2$ cup (65 g)	**Fresh blueberries**
$^1/_2$ cup (65 g)	**Fresh strawberries**

*P*reheat the oven to 375°F (180°C). Insert the garlic slivers into the racks of lamb and sprinkle with salt, pepper and fresh thyme. Sear in the citrus oil for 3 minutes over high heat. Finish cooking for 10 minutes in the oven.

During this time, in a saucepan, heat the port, maple syrup and red berry vinegar over medium heat. Gently incorporate the fresh fruit and simmer for about 5 minutes over medium heat, until the fruit begins to soften and abandon its flavor to the sauce.

Carve the pink racks of lamb, then arrange them on a large serving dish.

Cover with the delicious fruit fricassee and port. Supported by this lively and fruity sauce, the lamb will melt in your mouth and release magnificent flavors . . .

Calf's Liver
with Red Berry Compote

1	**Red onion, minced**
1	**White onion, minced**
2 tbsp (30 mL)	**Olive oil**
1 tbsp (15 g)	**Sugar**
8 tbsp (120 mL)	**Red berry vinegar**
1 cup (250 mL)	**Beef stock**
$^1/_2$ cup (65 g)	**Fresh or frozen strawberries**
4 x 5 oz (150 g)	**Calf's liver, sliced**
To taste	**Salt and ground pepper**

First, sweat and caramelize the onions for about 5 minutes over medium heat in the olive oil mixed with the sugar. Deglaze with $^1/_4$ cup (60 mL) of the red berry vinegar. Moisten with the beef stock, incorporate the fruit and reduce by half. Fry the liver slices over high heat, 1 minute per side. Deglaze with the remaining vinegar.

Serve immediately. Cover with the cooking liquid, and the fruit and onion compote.

The full-bodied, strong flavor of the liver will be judiciously underlined by this lively, tart sauce.

Hot Chèvre

with Red Berries and Spices

2	**Rolls of soft goat's milk cheese, halved**
2	**Shallots, finely chopped**
1 tbsp (15 mL)	**Olive oil**
1 tsp (5 g)	**Sugar**
$^1/_3$ cup (80 mL)	**Red berry vinegar**
1 Fruit	**Star anise**
1	**Cinnamon stick**
1	**Nutmeg clove**
$^1/_4$ cup (65 g)	**Raspberries**
$^1/_4$ cup (65 g)	**Cranberries**
$^1/_4$ cup (65 g)	**Blueberries**

First, caramelize the shallots over medium heat for at least 5 minutes in the olive oil and sugar. As the shallots cook, melt the goat's milk cheese sections by grilling in the oven for 3 to 4 minutes; do not allow them to stick.

Next, deglaze the shallots with the vinegar, then add the spices and fruit. Reduce over medium heat for 5 minutes until the fruit softens.

Cover the chèvre with this fruit purée. Accompany with some beautiful greens. Soft and creamy, and covered with this startling sauce, the goat's milk cheese will bloom in your mouth like a magnificent bouquet of flavors and aromas...

A Marriage
of Tastes

Vinaigrette,

mayonnaise

and

marinade

recipes

Even if the celebrated marriage between oil and vinegar is predictable, you can prevent it from sadly languishing by adding some creativity and innovation. Be daring and rekindle the flame by offering a few irresistible jewels. Spices, condiments, fruit juices or vegetable purées—any enticement is reason enough for embarking on an adventure that you will savor for a long time.

Pink Grapefruit and Ginger Vinaigrette

A flavored, fruity and smooth vinaigrette. Superb on endive, spinach and orange salads, or for marinating chicken breasts.

1	**Pink grapefruit (juice)**
1 $^1/4$ cup (300 mL)	**Citrus oil**
4 tbsp (60 mL)	**Soya sauce or tamari**
4 tbsp (60 mL)	**White wine vinegar**
2 tbsp (10 g)	**Fresh ginger, grated**
1 tbsp (15 mL)	**Honey**
To taste	**Salt and ground pepper**

Vigorously emulsify all the ingredients, using a whisk or a blender.

Orange-Flavored Vinaigrette

A fruity, tart and nicely flavored dressing... Superb on watercress or spinach salads, on radicchio or blanched fresh asparagus.

2 tbsp (30 mL)	**Dijon mustard**
1 tsp (5 g)	**Fresh or dried herbs**
To taste	**Salt and ground pepper**
1	**Orange (juice and zest)**
$^1/4$ cup (60 mL)	**Candied grape and tarragon vinegar (see page 159)**
2	**Green onions, finely minced**
1 cup (250 mL)	**Citrus oil**

In a food processor, incorporate the mustard, fresh or dried herbs, salt, pepper, orange juice and zest. Blend for a few seconds. Next, gently pour in the oil, while continuing to blend until a creamy vinaigrette is obtained. Then, add the vinegar and green onions. Blend for another few seconds and there you have it!

Olive and *Fines herbes* Vinaigrette

This seasoned and well-rounded vinaigrette will add a lot of taste to your crunchy greens, legume salads and hard-boiled eggs.

1 cup (250 mL)	**Anchoyade oil**
12	**Green olives, pitted**
$^1/3$ cup (85 mL)	**Garlic and basil vinegar**
2	**Garlic cloves, finely chopped**
2 tbsp (10 g)	**Fresh thyme, chopped**
To taste	**Salt and ground pepper**

Combine all the ingredients in a food processor until emulsified. You will have a well-rounded, Mediterranean-flavored vinaigrette... A delicious and surprising taste companion!

Creamy Tex-Mex Vinaigrette

Seasoned and delightfully spicy, this vinaigrette will energize and add character to your sandwiches and pasta, potato or avocado salads.

1 tbsp (15 mL)	**Maple syrup**
2 tbsp (30 mL)	**Tomato paste**
2 tbsp (30 mL)	**Garlic and basil vinegar**
2 tbsp (30 mL)	**Tex-Mex oil**
1 tbsp (15 mL)	**Worcestershire sauce**
1 cup (250 mL)	**Plain yogurt**
1 tsp (3 g)	**Fresh or dried herbs**
To taste	**Salt and ground pepper**

Using a whisk, thoroughly combine all the ingredients until a smooth and creamy vinaigrette is obtained.

Anchovy Vinaigrette

Magnificent on eggplant or grilled peppers, in a pepper salad, on crunchy greens with garlic croutons, or for marinating fish.

6	**Anchovy fillets**
1/2	**Lemon (juice)**
1	**Garlic clove, finely chopped**
2	**Green onions, finely chopped**
2 tbsp (30 mL)	**Dijon mustard**
2 tbsp (30 mL)	**Garlic and basil vinegar**
To taste	**Salt and ground pepper**
1 cup (250 mL)	**Anchoyade oil**

First, incorporate all the ingredients except the anchoyade oil in the blender. Blend for a few seconds, and add the oil in a thin stream, little by little, just as you would to prepare mayonnaise. Continue to blend until a creamy vinaigrette is obtained.

Cantonese Vinaigrette

A superb, sweet dressing. Delicious on warm fish, shrimp or scallop salads as well as on broccoli or green peas cooked al dente.

1/3 cup (80 mL)	**Oriental-flavored oil**
2/3 cup (160 mL)	**Sesame oil**
6 tbsp (90 mL)	**Soya sauce or tamari**
1 tbsp (15 mL)	**Honey**
1/4 cup (60 mL)	**Balsamic vinegar**
1 tbsp (5 g)	**Fresh ginger, grated**

Using a fork, or in the blender, vigorously emulsify this flavored vinaigrette.

198

Wild Berry Vinaigrette

Fruity, sweet and nervous, this vinaigrette will passionately season your bitter radicchio, chicory or endive salads. It is perfect with warm chicken or a confit of duck salad and can also serve as a marinade for chicken breasts.

1 cup (250 mL)	**Citrus oil**
4 tbsp (45 g)	**Raspberries**
2 tbsp (30 mL)	**Honey**
To taste	**Salt and ground pepper**
$^1/4$ cup (60 mL)	**Soya sauce or tamari**
$^1/4$ cup (60 mL)	**Raspberry vinegar**

In a food processor or blender, combine all these ingredients to prepare a colorful and flavorful vinaigrette.

Creamy Yogurt and Dill Vinaigrette

A fresh and tasty salad dressing that will happily accompany smoked or marinated fish or cucumber and potato salads.

1 cup (250 mL)	**Plain yogurt**
$^1/3$ cup (80 mL)	**Citrus oil**
2	**Garlic cloves, finely chopped**
1	**Lemon (juice and zest)**
4 tbsp (20 g)	**Fresh dill**
2 tbsp (10 g)	**Chives, finely chopped**
To taste	**Salt and ground pepper**

Combine all the ingredients in a blender to obtain a smooth and creamy dressing.

Old-Style Mustard Vinaigrette

This is a mellow, slightly sweet and tart vinaigrette, delicious on greens, tuna or chicken salad.

2 tbsp (30 mL)	**Dijon mustard**
$^1/3$ cup (80 mL)	**Grape and tarragon vinegar**
2 tbsp (30 mL)	**Maple syrup**
To taste	**Salt and ground pepper**
1 cup (250 mL)	*Fines herbes* **and shallot oil**

In a food processor, incorporate all the ingredients except the oil. Process for a few seconds. Next, add the oil in a thin stream, little by little, continuously blending until a creamy vinaigrette is obtained.

Hot Pepper Vinaigrette

This is a well-rounded, spicy and seasoned dressing that will add a lot of breadth to your eggplant purées, chickpea or fresh pasta salads.

1 cup (250 mL)	**Pepper oil**
2	**Garlic cloves, finely chopped**
2	**Green onions, finely chopped**
2	**Lemons (juice)**
2 tbsp (30 mL)	**Harissa sauce**
To taste	**Salt and ground pepper**

In a food processor or blender, combine all the ingredients to form a smooth, spicy and explosive vinaigrette!

Sun-Dried Tomato Coulis

Superbly flavored and colored for your spinach, pasta or potato salads, or to enhance the taste of Parma ham and olives.

1 cup (250 mL)	**Tomato juice**
1/3 cup (80 mL)	**Garlic and basil vinegar**
2	**Garlic cloves, crushed**
4	**Sun-dried tomatoes, finely chopped**
To taste	**Salt and ground pepper**

1 tbsp (10 g)	**Fresh basil**
2 tbsp (30 mL)	**Soya sauce or tamari**
1/2 cup (125 mL)	**Pomodoro oil**

In a blender, incorporate all the ingredients except the oil. Blend for a few seconds and add the oil in a thin stream, little by little, until a delicious and smooth vinaigrette is obtained.

Shallot and Honey Vinaigrette

A slightly bittersweet dressing with ample taste; marvelously accompanies radicchio, chicken and fresh pasta salads.

1 cup (250 mL)	***Fines herbes* and shallot oil**
2 tbsp (30 mL)	**Honey**
1	**Lemon (juice and zest)**
1	**Lime (juice and zest)**
1	**Garlic clove, crushed**
2 tbsp (30 g)	**Chives, finely chopped**

With a whisk or fork, vigorously emulsify all the ingredients to produce a refreshing vinaigrette.

Sweet Saffron Mayonnaise

2	Egg yolks
2 tbsp (30 mL)	Dijon mustard
1/2	Lemon (juice)
1/2 tbsp (5 g)	Saffron
To taste	Salt and ground pepper
1 2/3 cups (400 mL)	Saffron oil
2 tbsp (30 mL)	Garlic and basil oil
2 tbsp (30 mL)	Dry sherry

Nothing could be simpler than preparing this quick mayonnaise. Incorporate all the ingredients in the blender, except the oil, vinegar and sherry. Combine at medium speed, and incorporate the saffron oil in a thin stream until a creamy and delicious homemade mayonnaise is obtained. While continuing to blend, now add the vinegar and the hint of sherry. And, *voilà!*

Oriental-Flavored Mayonnaise

2	Egg yolks
2 tbsp (30 mL)	Dijon mustard
2 tbsp (30 mL)	Honey
To taste	Salt and ground pepper
1 2/3 cups (400 mL)	Oriental-flavored oil
1/2 tbsp (5 g)	Fresh ginger
3 1/2 tbsp (50 mL)	Balsamic vinegar
7 tbsp (110 mL)	Soya sauce or tamari

In a blender, incorporate all the ingredients except the oil, vinegar, soya sauce and fresh ginger. Blend at medium speed, and add the oil in a thin stream until a firm and flavored mayonnaise is obtained. While continuing to blend, add the ginger, balsamic vinegar and, lastly, the soya sauce. Blend for a few seconds more.

One-Minute Aïoli

2	Egg yolks
2 tbsp (30 mL)	Dijon mustard
1 2/3 cups (400 mL)	Anchoyade oil
1 tbsp (15 g)	Capers
1/2	Lemon (juice)
2 tbsp (30 mL)	Garlic and basil vinegar
4	Garlic cloves, crushed
To taste	Salt and ground pepper

Incorporate the egg and mustard. Blend at medium speed, and add the oil in a thin stream while continuing to blend; next, add the capers and remaining ingredients. Season to taste with salt and pepper.

Tartar Mayonnaise

2	**Egg yolks**
2 tbsp (30 mL)	**Dijon mustard**
2 tbsp (30 mL)	**Capers**
To taste	**Salt and ground pepper**
1 2/3 cups (400 mL)	**Citrus oil**
2 tbsp (10 g)	**Fresh Italian parsley, finely chopped**
2 tbsp (30 g)	**Pickled gherkins, minced**
1	**Shallot, finely chopped**
1/2	**Lemon (juice)**
2 tbsp (30 mL)	**Garlic and basil vinegar**

In a food processor, incorporate the egg yolks, mustard, capers, salt and pepper and blend at medium speed. While continuing to blend, incorporate the oil in a thin stream, then the parsley, gherkins, shallot, lemon juice and vinegar.

Pink Mayonnaise with Sun-Dried Tomatoes

2	**Egg yolks**
2	**Sun-dried tomatoes, rehydrated and minced**
2 tbsp (30 mL)	**Dijon mustard**
2	**Garlic cloves, crushed**
1 2/3 cups (400 mL)	**Pomodoro oil**
1/2	**Lemon (juice)**
2 tbsp (30 mL)	**Garlic and basil vinegar**
To taste	**Salt and ground pepper**

Incorporate the egg yolks, sun-dried tomatoes, Dijon mustard and garlic. Blend uniformly at medium speed. Next, while continuing to blend, add the oil in a thin stream, then the lemon juice and vinegar. Season to taste with salt and pepper. Blend until a pink and creamy mayonnaise is obtained.

Sweet Pepper Mayonnaise

2	**Egg yolks**
2 tbsp (30 mL)	**Dijon mustard**
1/2 cup (65 g)	**Red bell pepper, diced**
To taste	**Salt and ground pepper**
1 2/3 cups (400 mL)	**Pepper oil**
2 tbsp (30 mL)	**Garlic and basil vinegar**
1/2	**Lemon (juice)**

In a blender, incorporate the egg yolks, Dijon mustard, red pepper, salt and pepper. Combine at medium speed and add the oil in a thin stream while continuing to blend. Then, add the vinegar and lemon juice.

Cajun Marinade

1 can	Whole tomatoes (28 oz or 796 mL)
2 tbsp (30 mL)	Molasses
1/4 cup (60 mL)	Tex-Mex oil
2	Garlic cloves, crushed
1 tsp (5 g)	Paprika
4	Drops of green Tabasco sauce
To taste	Salt and ground pepper

In a food processor or blender, process all the ingredients to form a creamy purée. In a small, thick-bottomed saucepan, simmer the marinade and reduce by half over medium heat for about 10 minutes. Let cool before cheerfully using.

Santa Fe Marinade

4 tbsp (60 mL)	Liquid honey
1/4 cup (60 mL)	Soya sauce or tamari
1/3 cup (80 mL)	Garlic and basil vinegar
1/2 cup (125 mL)	Catsup
3	Garlic cloves, crushed
1/4 cup (60 mL)	Tex-Mex oil

In a large bowl, using a whisk, vigorously combine all the ingredients.

Dijon Mustard Marinade

4 tbsp (60 mL)	Dijon mustard
1 tbsp (10 g)	*Herbes de Provence*
3/4 cup (175 mL)	*Fines herbes* and shallot oil
2	Garlic cloves, crushed
2 tbsp (30 mL)	Liquid honey
1	Lemon (juice and zest)
To taste	Salt and ground pepper

Vigorously combine all the ingredients, using a whisk or fork.

Explosive Chili Marinade

3/4 cup (180 mL)	**Pepper oil**
4 tbsp (60 mL)	**Harissa sauce**
4 tbsp (60 mL)	**Tomato paste**
1	**Lemon (juice and zest)**
1	**Lime (juice and zest)**
2	**Garlic cloves, crushed**
1 tbsp (5 g)	**Thyme, chopped**
To taste	**Salt and ground pepper**

Combine all the ingredients to obtain a very spicy marinade.

Quick Oriental Marinade

1/2 cup (125 mL)	**Oriental-flavored oil**
1 cup (250 mL)	**Plain yogurt**
1	**Garlic clove, crushed**
2 tbsp (10 g)	**Fresh ginger, grated**
2 tbsp (10 g)	**Fresh coriander, finely chopped**
1	**Lemon (juice and zest)**
1 tbsp (5 g)	**Paprika**
To taste	**Salt and ground pepper**

Thoroughly combine all the ingredients, using a whisk or fork.

Pepper Duo Seasoned Marinade

3/4 cup (180 mL)	**Tex-Mex oil**
1/4 cup (60 mL)	**Garlic and basil vinegar**
2 tbsp (30 mL)	**Dijon mustard**
1 tbsp (15 g)	**Green peppercorns, in brine**
1 tbsp (15 g)	**Black pepper, freshly ground**
4 tbsp (60 mL)	**Catsup**
4 tbsp (60 mL)	**Tomato paste**
To taste	**Salt**

Process all the ingredients in the food processor or blender until a smooth marinade is obtained.

Citrus Fruit *Persillade*

1 cup (250 mL)	Citrus oil
2	Lemons (juice and zest)
2 tbsp (10 g)	Chives, finely chopped
2 tbsp (10 g)	Parsley, finely chopped
To taste	Salt and ground pepper

Thoroughly combine all the ingredients, using a whisk or fork.

Thai Curry and Coconut Marinade

2	Garlic cloves, pressed
1 tbsp (5 g)	Crushed chili
2 tbsp (5 g)	Curry powder
1/4 cup (60 mL)	Oriental-flavored oil
1 1/4 cups (315 mL)	Coconut milk
1	Lime (juice and zest)
1 dozen	Fresh basil leaves

First, heat the garlic, crushed chili and curry powder for a few seconds in the oil to release the flavors and aromas. Add the coconut milk, lime juice and zest. Heat over medium heat for about 5 minutes. Add the basil at the last minute. Then, in a food processor or blender, process until a smooth and creamy dressing is obtained.

Bittersweet Peach Marinade

1 can	Peaches in syrup, well drained
1/4 cup (60 mL)	Tex-Mex oil
4 tbsp (60 mL)	Liquid honey
To taste	Salt and ground pepper
1/2 cup (125 mL)	Exotic fruit vinegar
1/3 cup (80 mL)	Soya sauce or tamari

In a small, thick-bottomed saucepan, brown and caramelize the peaches in the Tex-Mex oil and honey. Season to taste with salt and pepper, deglaze with the vinegar and immediately moisten with the soya sauce. Reduce for 1 to 2 minutes, then process in a food processor until a beautiful purée is obtained. Reduce again in a small, thick-bottomed saucepan, about 5 minutes over medium heat.

Citrus Fruit and Ginger Marinade

1/2 cup (100 mL)	Citrus oil
1 tbsp (5 g)	Fresh ginger, grated
1/3 cup (80 mL)	Soya sauce or tamari
1	Lemon (juice and zest)
2 tbsp (30 mL)	Liquid honey
To taste	Salt and ground pepper

Incorporate all the ingredients in the blender to prepare an exotic marinade.

CHIARELLO, Michael. *Flavored Oils.* San Francisco: Chronicle, 1995.

COURTINE, Robert, J., ed. *Larousse Gastronomique.* Paris: Éditions Larousse, 1984.

FLAVIGNY, Laure, ed. *Larousse de la cuisine.* Paris: Éditions Larousse, 1990.

HALM, Meesha. *The Balsamic Vinegar Cookbook.* San Francisco: HarperCollins, 1996.

LAMBERT-LAGACÉ, Louise, and Michelle LAFLAMME. *Bon gras, mauvais gras. Une question de santé.* Montreal: Éditions de l'Homme, 1993.

MONETTE, Solange. *Le nouveau Dictionnaire des aliments.* Montreal: Éditions Québec-Amérique, 1996.

PLANTE, Jean-François. *Simplement gourmand.* Montreal: Éditions Communiplex, 1995.

RIDGWAY, Judy. *Le guide de l'huile d'olive.* Courevoie: Éditions Soline, 1996.

SCOTTO, Élisabeth, and Brigitte FORGEUR. *L'huile d'olive.* Paris: Éditions du Chêne, 1995.

Oils

Vinegars

Recipes

Jean-François Plante would like to thank the enthusiastic team that worked with him in preparing this work, in particular:

Annick Loupias, editor,
for his overwhelming enthusiasm, his availability, understanding and his concern for just the right word;

Pierre Lafrenière, photographer,
for his immense talent and his love of light;

Jacques Faucher, chef,
for his gentle craziness, creativity, magic touch and formidable taste buds;

Renée Girard, stylist,
for her warm presence, and the fine and nuanced touch that she brings to every photo.

He would also like to highlight the remarkable efforts of the team at Éditions de l'Homme, in particular that of:

Josée Amyotte, layout and graphic designer,
for her unbridled imagination, inimitable touch and perfectionism;

Mélanie Sabourin, photo processing technician,
for the care she took to nourish the soul of each photo;

Céline Bouchard, proofreader,
for her gentle manner and infinite patience.